Wendy Michaels & Maureen Walsh

UP & AWAY

Using
Picture
Books

OXFORD
UNIVERSITY PRESS

Dedication

Look upon a little child
For my mother
who showed me, as a little child,
the value of
words and pictures and stories.

WM

For Sean

MW

OXFORD UNIVERSITY PRESS AUSTRALIA

Oxford   New York   Toronto
Delhi Bombay Calcutta Madras Karachi
Petaling Jaya Singapore Hong Kong Tokyo
Nairobi Dar es Salaam Cape Town
Melbourne Auckland
and associated companies in
Berlin   Ibadan

OXFORD is a trade mark of Oxford University Press

© Wendy Michaels and Maureen Walsh 1990
First published 1990
Reprinted 1990

National Library of Australia
Cataloguing-in-Publication data:

Michaels, Wendy.
   Up and away: using picture books.

   Bibliography.
   Includes indexes.
   ISBN 0 19 553139 6.

   1. Picture-books for children—Educational aspects.
   [2]. Language arts (Primary). 3. Language arts
   (Secondary). I. Walsh, Maureen.
   II. Title.

371.32

Designed by Steve Randles
Typeset by Solo Typesetting, South Australia
Printed by Impact Printing, Melbourne
Published by Oxford University Press,
253 Normanby Road, South Melbourne, Australia

Contents

Foreword

The sharing of a picture book involves students in the processes of speaking and listening. Picture books tend, by their very nature, to be read aloud by one person to a group of people. They invite discussion and verbal response. The process of reading involves far more than simply decoding words. The pictures themselves need to be 'read', involving close and careful observation and refining of these observations. Moreover, picture books with their essentially compact and carefully structured language provide useful models for further writing activities.

Students today live in a visual world. The mass media rely heavily on visual images as the most important coding device for their messages. It is vital that our students are taught to decode pictures in the same way that they are taught to decode verbal texts. Furthermore, there is a complex interrelationship between words and pictures in the telling of a story that can have implications for the nature of the communication.

In the reading and sharing of a picture book the similarities and differences between oral and written language are highlighted. This is an important part of the language learning of students—a difference that is all too often glossed over in the teaching of English in the classroom.

This in itself would be sufficient to justify the use of picture books in all classrooms. In addition to this, the picture book has developed in a way that makes it one of the most complex of modern literary genres. The study of the ways in which the language codes of words and pictures can interact and intersect to form a continuous narrative is a worthwhile study in itself. Some of the changes that have taken place in the picture book genre may well have been stimulated by the changing technology of the mass media. Such techniques as flashbacks have been adapted for the picture book by writers such as John Burningham.

The picture book, as a literary genre, is also a very effective tool in the learning process, as it provides suitable contexts for the exploration of reflection upon learning. This is particularly true of the reading/writing processes. Picture books slow down the reading process so that students are able to become reflective, in the way that Jack Thompson (1987) advocates in his study *Understanding Teenagers Reading*.

Contemporary curriculum documents in English focus on the need for an integrated approach to the study of language. The Victorian curriculum document 'English Study Design' stresses the need for 'students to regard reading, writing, listening, speaking and thinking as active and integrated processes' (Victorian Curriculum and Assessment Board 1989). The NSW Years 7–10 English Syllabus states that 'learning for the most part occurs as students use language, as they talk, listen, read, write, observe and reflect upon the processes of their own learning' (NSW Board of Secondary Education 1987); and the NSW 2 Unit Contemporary English Syllabus document asserts that 'speaking and listening, reading and writing should be taught as interrelated aspects of language, but teaching programs should also focus on the differences between these language modes' (NSW Board of Secondary Education 1988). While there are many contexts within which these objectives can be realised, the picture book provides one of the most compact and complex contexts for such integrated study.

This book explores these issues and provides the teacher with a wealth of approaches and activities, including reproducible pages, that can be used successfully within any classroom.

Acknowledgement

We gratefully acknowledge and warmly thank Maya Cranitch for the invaluable contribution to the Aboriginal Stories section.

Picture Books

Once upon a time picture books were considered to be merely children's books. Indeed they were largely intended for a young audience. They told tales that appeared to be simple, and were constructed so that the story was enlivened by pictures. Presumably, the assumption underlying such books was that children would not sustain an interest in the story unless there were some accompanying visual stimuli. Whether this is true or not (and we now doubt that this is the case), for many years picture books have been confined to the menu of younger children. Picture books published as literature have generally been classified as being for young readers. Basal reading schemes employ pictures as part of their attempt to foster word recognition skills—a practice which has further reinforced the notion that pictures are for beginning readers. The obvious corollary to this has been that once children can read they are no longer in need of pictures to assist them, and consequently books for older readers have been generally published without such graphic elements.

Pictures and picture books are not only appropriate to younger or beginning readers as aids to learning reading, but are an important part of the meaning-making process. Reading pictures is just as complex, perhaps more complex, than reading print: it can also be just as rewarding as reading print. When the two symbolic systems work together the satisfaction, enjoyment and stimulation is more than doubled. Like print, pictures are meaning systems, and it is important that we learn to unravel the meanings that are contained within them. It is equally important that we learn to acknowledge the ways in which these two symbolic meaning systems can work together.

Today, visual stimuli, in the form of pictographs of various kinds, regulate much of our communication with one another. Consider a newspaper without the political or social commentary carried in the cartoon. Consider an advertisement without visual imagery. Consider almost any form of media communication without a visual component.

In a world that relies increasingly on visual means of communication, picture books have established themselves as a complex literary genre, in which both verbal and visual cues structure meaning. Certainly some picture books have an appeal to very young children. Certainly some picture books are more appropriate to a child audience. However it is no longer true to assume this for all picture books. Both in structure and in content picture books are spread over a wide range of age groupings.

Good picture books are not trite, simple or juvenile. Picture books available today cover a range of topics that have universal significance: sibling rivalry, time passing, war, nuclear holocaust, death and a variety of political statements. Picture books offer humour, irony, poetry, good stories well told, social criticism and deep psychological insights. Moreover, they offer readers ways of 'getting into the story' by 'wandering around inside the picture'.

It is not only the content that has developed within the picture book genre. The structure of picture books has also developed in diverse ways. Where we might once have thought of picture books either as picture/caption books, or as stories with significant parts of the verbal text reproduced in visual form, we now find that some picture books have evolved into complex structures that require readers to fill in gaps in the text in a variety of exciting ways. Even where the picture/caption-type books still appear, as in many of the alphabet-style books, there are dense layers within the visual text that challenge competent readers. The illustrated book has similarly developed in such a way that it offers readers new and vital challenges.

The enormous development within picture books that has occurred over the last decade or so has firmly established the picture book as a legitimate literary genre. When we consider particular picture books it is obvious that there are a number of sub-genres within this general category. Not all picture books work in the same way. At one extreme there are picture books which contain no verbal text, and at the other extreme there are picture books with large amounts of verbal text, and pictures which seem almost incidental to the story. We have identified six main sub-genres of picture book:

- artbooks
- dual narratives
- cartoons/comics
- illustrated
- interactive
- wordless

This is not an exhaustive list: we have been deliberately selective. Our aim is to provide teachers of upper primary and secondary English with a background of literary knowledge that will assist them in choosing picture books suitable for the literary studies of their classrooms. We have therefore omitted picture/caption books (although that must not be construed as a statement of their lack of value), and the wide variety of picture books in the expository mode currently on the market. We also need to consider that this is a developing genre, and that new ways of structuring text may well be developed in the near future. What we offer here is a discussion of those texts to which we believe students should be exposed in the course of their literary studies.

ARTBOOKS

This sub-genre of picture books is distinguished by an emphasis on illustrations, almost to the exclusion of any verbal text. The pictures present some often ingenious art forms that might highlight particular techniques. Such books may indeed make some strong statements, but tend not to have a strong narrative flow, with little reliance on particular characters and little real conflict that involves readers in empathising with a character or situation. Very often the verbal text is used as a caption for the pictures, and sometimes the pictures may be very loosely connected. Traditional rhymes and poems are often used as the stimulus for these books, the words being so well known that they tend not to be reread. It is the illustrations that readers are concerned with.

Wild Animals by Brian Wildsmith.

Australian ballads have been used extensively in this way. Sometimes this has involved printing songs such as 'Click go the Shears' and other well-known ballads, accompanied by reproductions of classic paintings by painters such as Tom Roberts or Pro Hart. These picture books, attractive to the tourist industry, celebrate something of the heritage of the bush ethos — as the dust cover of one such publication asserts, 'a jubilant celebration of a tough way of life and of men who were tough enough to live it and tender enough to sing about it'. These books are effectively authorless as they represent the work of other writers and artists assembled by an editor or publisher.

Some illustrators, however, use the words of existing poems or songs and present these with original illustrations. Here we have a reinterpretation of the known words through the eyes of the artist. This offers readers the opportunity of rereading the known with fresh insights. Desmond Digby's *Waltzing Matilda* is a prime example of this. Digby takes the story of the swagman and gives it new life by placing him within the Australian landscape. Digby's illustrations capture the colour and texture of the Australian sheep country. There are light-hearted touches within the illustrations: for instance, when the policemen arrive, 'one, two and three', Digby echoes their numbers in the trees, rocks, sheep and the galahs.

The illustrations in these books generally fill the entire page or double page. They are usually extremely colourful and often very detailed and intricate. This is the case with Graeme Base's *Animalia* which is in effect an elaborate picture alphabet book. Each page depicts fantastic creatures and objects whose names commence with the given letter, and is captioned by a highly alliterative phrase, such as 'diabolical dragons daintily devouring delicious delicacies' and 'ingenious iguanas improvising an intricate impromptu on impossibly impractical instruments'.

Brian Wildsmith produces similar work in his books *Wild Animals* and *What the Moon Saw*. The former consists of full-page colour illustrations of animals with captions such as 'a herd of elephants' and 'an ambush of tigers'. The latter has a thinly veiled narrative consisting of a conversation between the moon and the sun. This narrative does not really develop beyond picture captioning, reminiscent of basal reading schemes, with sentences such as 'Here is a fat hippopotamus, and there is a thin lizard', with the words 'fat' and 'thin' highlighted in bold type. These captioning sentences run in a thin band across the pages which are filled with the colour illustrations.

Betty Young's *Pink Pigs in Mud* also employs this technique. This book consists of photographs of the fine embroidery work of Betty Young. The verbal text consists of one sentence, with one phrase appearing on each consecutive page, and a question addressed directly to the reader on the last page: 'Which colours can you see in this picture?' Each page contains a predominant colour, and that colour is repeated in the text.

Loosely connected narrative seems to be the predominant feature of these books. Very often readers may be forgiven for assuming that the narrative has been constructed after the artwork and has very little real connection with it. This is certainly the case with the work of Ann Jonas in *Round Trip* and *Reflections*. The former consists of a trip into the city and back again. Even though the story is told in the first person plural, we have absolutely no sense of the characters in this book. The book consists of a series of pictures which readers follow through in the normal fashion until on the last page they read: 'We watched as the sun set. Time to turn around.' The book is then turned upside-down and the story of the return journey appears. The black and white illustrations work in reverse as different scenes. This somewhat ingenious means of constructing the pictures works quite well from a distance, but is not as convincing on close examination. The verbal text is trite and tends to work almost as a distraction from the pictures: 'In the country, telephone poles lined the road.' *Reflections* works on a similar principle, although in this case the illustrations are in colour. This story is told in the first person singular, but once again there is little sense of the character. The verbal text is primarily picture captioning, with no sense of what the character is feeling or thinking at all: 'Sometimes a storm comes up on the bay. It rains for a while. Then the sun comes out again.' These texts do not really invite readers into the text, primarily because the narrative is constructed with such gaucherie.

There are a number of books that fall into this category of artbooks, not necessarily because they highlight illustrations, but rather because they use the art of the book as the basis of their text. The most obvious of these are the many pop-up books that have recently regained popularity. Again, these books are not always concerned with a strong narrative that invites readers to identify with characters in their conflicts. The pop-up may have a distancing effect, constantly reminding readers that they are in fact reading a book. Mitsumasa

Anno has used this device in what is basically an expository text in *The Earth is a Sundial*. Here the pop-ups illustrate in a three-dimensional way the information that is being presented in the text.

As well as pop-up books there are books which employ cut-outs so that the layers of pictures are seen through from one page to the next. This may be well integrated into the story as in *The Very Hungry Caterpillar*, or it may be merely an addendum to the story, as in *Pigs Might Fly* by Liz Underhill. Here the cut-outs tend to show us what is happening through a window. Thus the words, 'Leaning through the hatch, he ordered two Stoat House Specials . . .' are accompanied by a picture of the hatch cut out to reveal what is happening in the kitchen.

Fold-outs may also be part of this sub-genre of picture books. Where such techniques predominate there tends to be only a slight narrative. Such devices again underline that this is a construct, and they do tend to distance the readers' involvement in the issues of the story as they become more concerned with the device itself. In Eric Carle's *Papa, please get the moon for me*, not only do we have paintings that look very much like those of an infant, painted in poster paints with a thick brush, but the paintings extend beyond the page so that the reader must fold out the illustrations. The direction of the fold depends on the action in the picture. Thus, when the father is getting a long ladder, the page folds out sideways; when he stands the ladder up to climb to the moon, the page opens upwards; when he reaches the moon, it opens both top and bottom; and when he is climbing down, it opens downwards. There is little text beyond the sort of captioning of 'Down and down and down he climbed', and 'She hugged the moon and threw it into the air' — actions which are in fact shown in the pictures.

The manipulation of artistic devices and structures can create interesting narratives where the text is sufficiently dense. The work of Janet and Allan Ahlberg amply illustrates this, particularly in the delightful book *The Jolly Postman or Other People's Letters*. In this text there is a thin narrative thread of a postman who delivers letters to a number of characters. These characters are linked through their existence in traditional fairy tales. Thus readers need to know the tales in order to understand the allusions. What makes this story even more dense is that as the postman stops at each house, or palace, the readers are able to open the envelope that is part of the text and read the letter contained in it. The letters are varied: a birthday card for Goldilocks; an advertisement for Hobgoblin supplies for the Witch; a solicitor's letter to the Wolf who is occupying Grandma's cottage, and so on. The narrative winds its way along with the postman, beginning with Goldilocks' letter of apology to the Three Bears and ending with her birthday card. This framework, along with the allusions to the traditional tales, maintains a much more tightly structured narrative than in many books within this category.

DUAL NARRATIVE

In this style of picture book there are, in effect, two different narratives happening simultaneously. They are connected through the interaction of the words and the pictures, yet there is often a very subtle and wry humour created by the differing perspectives of the narrator in the verbal text, and the narrator in the visual text. Readers of this style of text must continually shift between these two perspectives. Very often the text carries what appears to be a very simple story line. It is in the visual that the layers of meaning are contained.

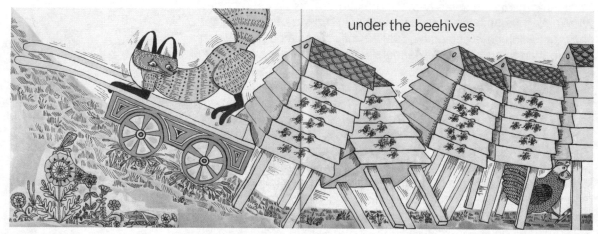

under the beehives

Rosie's Walk by Pat Hutchins.

The apparent simplicity of these dual narrative books makes them ideal to read to younger children, while at the same time offering more advanced readers the opportunity to explore differing perspectives. Pat Hutchins' *Rosie's Walk*, for instance is an apparently simple tale of a hen who takes a walk around the farmyard and arrives home 'in time for tea'. In fact, the verbal narrative is told through one sentence, with one phrase appearing on each page. The visual narrative, however, shows the real events of Rosie's walk. As she meanders through the farmyard she is pursued by a fox. This is not, of course, mentioned in the verbal narrative. The fox is less than fortunate in his attempts to catch the hen: on each page he attempts to pounce on Rosie, but she evades capture through a variety of fortuitous events that leave the fox in most uncomfortable situations. The real subtlety of this story is that the reader cannot be sure whether Rosie is aware of the fox's presence or not. The reader is left wondering just how many of the fox's accidents were deliberately engineered by Rosie.

While *Rosie's Walk* has become a classic of this style of picture book, there are others that work in similar ways. Jan Ormerod's *The Story of Chicken Licken* is another text where two separate narratives are operating simultaneously. The story of Chicken Licken is being performed by a group of school children on a stage in what appears to be the school hall. While this story is being played out on the stage in the light, the readers also witness another story happening in the shadows among the audience. The readers of the book seem to be seated with these people in the audience. This story is told through the visual text. We see a baby climb out of a bassinet, pull the papers out of a briefcase, and crawl along the floor, up the steps at the side of the stage, and onto the platform. We also see another member of the audience fall asleep and a mother hush a noisy child. The two stories come together when the lights come on in the auditorium to reveal the havoc that the crawling baby has caused. The baby has been retrieved by a sibling who was playing a part in the play.

While there appears to be a simplicity in these stories individually, the complex interweaving of the dual narrative creates a gentle humour and rewards attentive readers.

COMIC OR CARTOON-STYLE PICTURE BOOKS

There has been a proliferation of picture books that tell their tale through the use of the comic format. Here we have a number of sequent frames, as used in some of the wordless picture books. However, we also have the complication of dialogue and thoughts provided in balloons, and often the addition of a narrator's voice in the form of captions. Readers need to be very active in reading this sort of text. They must read each picture, the words of the dialogue and the caption in conjunction with each other. Moreover these texts very often contain a large number of frames on the one page, and use a variety of sizes for the frames. The need to make these frequent shifts tends to 'alienate' readers, in the Brechtian sense. The obvious unreality of this genre assists the reader in the process of 'willing suspension of disbelief'. Within this genre animals can talk to humans; time and place can shift; dreams and thoughts can be shown contemporaneously with actions; events can be highly improbable; characters can be truly unreal. It is difficult to empathise with any particular character in these stories, but on the other hand it is very easy to ponder the issues being presented.

It is not surprising, therefore, to find that many books of this type deal with very important and vital human issues. Fears, things that go bump in the night, death and nuclear war are among the topics that have been tackled through picture comic books. Posy Simmonds' book *Fred* explores the reactions of two children and all the neighbourhood cats to the death of the cat Fred. The cartoons show the importance of dealing with the death and loss in an honest way, without euphemism. Raymond Briggs' *When the Wind Blows* deals with the issue of nuclear

Fred by Posy Simmons.

war and the tragedy of believing that there is any possibility of survival. The importance of this issue is highlighted through the cartoon characters and particularly through the smallness of the cartoons that depict the activities of James and his wife, juxtaposed with the double-page spreads that depict the missiles and the blast.

Some comic picture books do deal with less weighty subjects. There may be a more gently ironic lampooning of social issues. This is the case with some of the work of Raymond Briggs. In *Fungus the Bogeyman* Briggs satirises many social mores, conventions and values, from cleanliness through to the 'richness of our literary heritage'. In *Father Christmas Goes on Holiday* he gently lampoons the British, French, Scottish, and Americans as well as the behaviour of those on holiday. This gentle irony allows us to laugh at the foibles without deep emotional attachment.

Some recent comic picture books show the influence of the television cartoon in their format. This appears not only in their content, but also in the visual and verbal text. The verbal text has something of the intensity of the human voice-over that often accompanies television cartoons, using the present tense to suggest immediacy, and incorporating onomatopoeic words such as 'zap' within the pictures. The pictures in this sort of book are very busy with a great deal of colour and an enormous amount of action happening within each frame. Colin Hawkins' *Cosmic Cat* books are examples of this sort of text. Even the title page of *Cosmic Cat and the Pink Planet* is reminiscent of the credits of a television cartoon, with all the characters identified both visually and verbally, including a new character—'. . . and introducing DAARG, a jungle hero'.

A simpler form of the comic picture book is found in some texts where each page is in effect a frame. Here there is usually no narrator, but the characters' dialogue is presented in balloons, and the sequence of the narrative is carried through the pictures. In a delightful little tale, *Don't Forget the Bacon*, Pat Hutchins uses this technique to explore what goes on inside the mind. The child in this story is sent to the shops with a list of purchases and the remonstrance 'don't forget the bacon'. As readers follow him on his journey they see through the balloons how the words in his mind become associated with the things that he is observing on the way. Needless to say he does forget the bacon amidst the jumble of other things that are happening in his head.

Comic-style picture books allow readers to distance themselves from a close emotional involvement in characters and examine the issues or ideas that are presented. Readers of the comic picture book must be prepared to work hard, following the thread of the narrative from differing perspectives.

ILLUSTRATED PICTURE BOOKS

Books in which the flow of the narrative is carried primarily through the verbal text, but which contain some accompanying illustrations, fall into the category of illustrated picture books. Many of these are retellings of old folk tales, particularly those of the Brothers Grimm. Others are representations of well-known poems or nursery rhymes. There are also a number of illustrated picture books that tell new stories, and very often these have the quality of myth or legend about them. Some of these books have a lot of writing on the page, and some have pages without pictures at all.

These books can be read without 'reading' the pictures and still maintain the flow of the narrative, but that does not mean that the pictures are redundant. On the contrary, the pictures work with the text in a variety of ways.

The pictures in some illustrated picture books may elaborate upon the verbal text, providing details of setting which are not given in the verbal text. In this way they act as a backdrop to the story, as a scenic painting does in a play. The reader uses the illustrations to fill in the gaps in the verbal text. Ruth Brown's retelling of *A Dark Dark Tale* contains this type of illustration. In the opening picture, we see on the 'moor' a number of rabbits hiding in clumps of grass and an owl swooping over them. Later in the 'hall' we see cobwebs, statues of mythical animals, the bust of a man, a set of three stained glass windows, and a black cat slinking up the stairs. As the story progresses, more complex elements are introduced into the illustrations. For instance, the 'curtain' contains patterns of faces with peering eyes. This is then picked up in the faces of the dolls in the 'cupboard'. Thus the illustrations allow readers to elaborate upon the simple text, and to fill in quite complex details.

The illustrations assist readers in constructing the narrative's setting, particularly where the settings are in foreign or distant climes. The illustrations fill in the gaps and make visible for readers those details of setting which the verbal text does not, or cannot, provide. For instance, in the retelling of the story of *Louhi* by Toni de Gerez, the illustrations depict the landscape of Finland with its log cabins, high mountains, forests and snow. There is a full-page illustration of Seppo, the blacksmith, at work. Arlene Mosel's retelling of *Tikki Tikki Tembo* similarly sets the scene of this story in China, providing readers with pictorial information that is assumed in the verbal text. This is also the case with Junko Morimoto's tale of *The White Crane*. One illustration depicts the kind of 'fire' that is referred to in the text — the open indoor fire of the Japanese house.

There are many tales from other cultures told through illustrated picture books. These do not always have realistic representations of the landscapes in their illustrations. Sometimes the illustrations are symbolic or imagistic. Readers use these to enlarge on the text, but also to gain some feeling for the cultural diversity within the story. This is true of most of the Aboriginal tales of Dick Roughsey, in which the illustrations draw on the traditions of Aboriginal art, transposed into a white context. Similarly, *Arrow to the Sun* by Gerald McDermott draws on the traditions of the Pueblo Indians, and *Death of the Iron Horse* by Paul Goble shows the influence of the Cheyenne Indians' art traditions. Traditional forms of Japanese art are found in *The Painter and the Wild Swans* by Claude Clement, *The Hiroshima Story* by Toshi Maruki, and *The Inch Boy* by Junko Morimoto. In each of these books, the illustrations add to the narrative by providing a cultural landscape against which readers construct the story.

In retelling traditional tales the writer and illustrator often manipulate the illustrations to work as a counterpoint to the verbal text, commenting on the narrative. One of the finest examples of this is the retelling of *Hansel and Gretel* by Anthony Browne. The verbal text tells the story in a traditional style, but the illustrations set the tale at the edge of a forest in the twentieth century. Through this juxtaposition the readers are invited to see the story as both legendary and contemporary. As the verbal text tells of the famine and the suffering of the family through their lack of food, we are shown through the illustrations the greed and avarice of the step-mother with her abundance of cosmetics, perfumes and other such frivolities. We also see the connection between the step-mother and the wicked witch, through Browne's careful manipulation of shadows around the step-mother that are in the shape of a witch's hat. The readers must follow the images within the illustrations to gain the full message of this story.

In retelling traditional tales authors sometimes choose to alter or twist the tale, and to use a caricature format for illustrations. This immediately signals to the readers that this is a piece of satire. Tony Ross has established himself as a master of this style. Ross takes traditional fables or moral tales that are deliberately didactic and lampoons the tale through his illustrations. *Foxy Fables* and *The Boy Who Cried Wolf* are two examples of his work. In the latter the Wolf is represented in the attire of an elite gentleman in coat and tails who has every concern for proper etiquette. This works against the fact that people would provide his normal diet. The cartoon-like drawings clearly point out this irony.

Hansel and Gretel illustrated by Anthony Browne.

New tales told through the illustrated picture book may use the visual text to amplify key images within the narrative. The images may be incorporated within whole illustrations, or may be isolated on the page without a frame. In *Piggybook*, Anthony Browne uses the recurring image of a pig to make his point about the lifestyle of the males of this story. The pig image appears in shadows, on the wallpaper, in close-ups of sausages, in piggybanks, on doorknobs, on the clockface and even on the face of the moon. This imagery is echoed in the text where verbs suggestive of pigs, such as 'grunted', 'squealed', and 'snorted', are used to describe the behaviour of these males. Browne uses a similar device in *The Visitors Who Came to Stay*. Here images which appear in the main illustrations also appear in isolation on the pages containing the verbal text. The boiled egg which turns to a fried egg with 'black frills' is one such image. Shells, sweets, shoes and fruit all assume a symbolic significance as the story progresses. Another image which is isolated is that of the sea and sky in the shape of a question mark. This image synthesises the key idea of this book.

A further category of illustrated picture books is closely related to the novella. These generally have quite a lengthy verbal text, which can be dense and poetic in quality. Within these texts there are often illustrations of a highly artistic nature which tend to be interspersed within the text in a symbolic way. Sometimes they depict the setting of the story, or a specific character, or a particular incident or event. Essentially what these pictures contribute to the narrative is the sense of mood or tone, reinforcing the epic nature of the story. Leon Garfield's tale *The Wedding Ghost*, illustrated by Charles Keeping, is an example of this style of picture book. The pen and ink drawings interspersed through the verbal text reinforce the sinister and sombre mood. In Joan Aiken and Alan Lee's *The Moon's Revenge* the illustrations assist readers in establishing the changes in mood as the threat of the monster looms. Other illustrations highlight some of the significant events such as the making of the fiddle and the throwing of the shoes at the moon. Aiken and Lee use a similar style in *The Mirrorstone*. Within this text they also incorporate holograms that give the illustrations a three-dimensional quality. *Farmer Schulz's Ducks* by Colin Thiele is another tale that uses fine watercolour paintings both to set the scene and to highlight significant events such as the ducks crossing the bridge.

At the other extreme is the style of illustrated picture book in which the illustrations dominate the page and the verbal text acts almost as a caption to them. It is possible to read this type of story without the pictures, and equally it is almost possible to 'read' the story without the words. Robert Roennfeldt's adaptation of *Tiddalick* uses this format with cartoon-like drawings. Chana Byers Abells' *The Children We Remember* uses photographs to depict the story of the Holocaust, with very simple text captioning. The mood and tone of these books is largely derived from the pictures, while the simple verbal text relates the events.

INTERACTIVE PICTURE BOOKS

There are many picture books in which the narrative flow is carried by the close and intricate interaction of the visual and verbal text. The two aspects of the narrative are inextricably linked in such a way that it is virtually impossible to read one without the other. Picture books which operate in this way can offer readers a density and complexity that may not be found in the other types of picture books. Readers have to recognise the pattern of the interaction and move in and out of the two symbolic systems in order to create the meaning. There are a variety of ways in which the narrative flow can move between the two types of symbolic representation.

Where the wild things are *eg*

There may be a very direct connection between visual and verbal text, with the words pointing readers to the pictures. The readers must move from the words to the pictures and then on to the next set of words. This happens in the delightful little book by Janet and Allan Ahlberg, *Each Peach Pear Plum*. On the title page readers are invited to play 'I spy' with the text that follows. The book is arranged in such a way that the words, in the form of a single rhyming couplet, are on the left-hand page, accompanied by an illustration that links with the words on the opposite page. The words direct readers to search out a 'hidden meaning' (literally) in the picture. Thus, the first page invites readers to find Tom Thumb who is hiding in the peach tree in the orchard. The illustration on the left-hand page is of a peach, a pear, a plum, and Tom Thumb's hat. This pattern is repeated as the page is turned, with the word on the next page being added to the picture on the right-hand page. On the page following Mother Hubbard we meet Cinderella. The left-hand page shows her broom, a stool and a mouse. The right-hand page reveals only her arm in the process of dusting the cellar. The illustrations have a delightful 'olde worlde' charm reminiscent of the early illustrated picture books of Mother Goose.

This little book is, of course, heavily inter-textual. It sets up a repeated pattern using symbols associated with each nursery rhyme character or legendary figure. This encourages readers to predict and anticipate, and rewards readers for doing this on the last page, where the last word of the rhyming couplet — 'everyone' — is left to a page of its own, creating a gentle climactic effect. There is a comic final page with an illustration of the empty pie dish being scavenged by two rabbits and a bird.

The narrative may alternate between the pictures and the words but the readers' attention may not be drawn directly to it through the words. The readers may be left to deduce the connection through a reading of the pictures. Pat Hutchins uses this technique in *The Wind Blew*. There is a simple verbal text which, except for the first and the last lines, consists of rhyming couplets. However this book begins with a picture and the words follow this. This pattern is repeated for a number of pages with the left-hand page advancing the story and the words following after the events. All the new characters are introduced before the words tell us what is to happen to them. Thus we see

Priscilla with her balloon on the page prior to the words that tell us what is to happen to her. This repeated pattern once again allows readers to anticipate each new stage of the narrative from the visual images, and the words confirm their predictions.

Another way in which the visual and verbal elements of the text may interact is related to the comic book, with elements of the verbal text being incorporated within the illustrations. This may happen in the form of balloons containing the characters' words. In *What's that Noise?* the sounds of the animals, 'hiss', 'squawk', 'growl', and 'shriek', are simply represented within the illustrations. Such a device may become part of an overall symbolic pattern. Pamela Allen uses this technique particularly effectively in the book *Bertie and the Bear*. Here, is a simple story line that involves a bear who is chasing Bertie, and who has attracted the attention of a hierarchy of characters from the Queen to the little dog, each joining in the chase and making their own particular noise. The words of the narrative generally appear on the left-hand page. The pictures spread across both pages, and part of the picture on each page consists of the noise that the character makes in the chase. Not only is this noise—'shoo shoo you monster you', 'blah blah', 'bong ong', etc—repeated in a balloon on the adjacent page, but each noise is given a colour which eventually takes on symbolic significance. The chase halts for two pages as the bear takes a bow and begins to dance, and the pictures take up the narrative of the dance. Six pictures show the bear's dance prowess. As the remainder of the chasers join in the dance, the colours and noise which they had previously been making in a discordant fashion is melded together into the harmony of the rainbow, and the discord disappears. The colours are revealed to be the colours that make up the rainbow and thus their symbolic significance is revealed.

The interaction between words and pictures can be quite complex. The pictures on adjacent pages might fill in the gaps between the words, illustrating the 'sub-textual' levels of meaning. This is very common in the work of Maurice Sendak, particularly in *Where the Wild Things Are*. This book employs a compact verbal text juxtaposed with pictures in a crosshatched style which suggests layers of meaning. The words in the text are elaborated upon within the illustrations. For instance, the 'mischief of one kind and another' is shown through the pictures of Max chasing the dog and hanging up teddy by one arm. In Anthony Browne's *Gorilla* the movie that Hannah and the Gorilla see is shown through the picture rather than in words. In Sendak's *Outside Over There*, layers of meaning are carried through the illustrations, particularly the window scenes which reflect what Ida is thinking or imagining. The pictures here are an integral part of the story. The flow of the narrative depends upon the reader moving in and out of the pictures and words.

In some texts the narrative flow may move from words to pictures. Here the narrative may begin with words or with words and pictures, but the pictures may take over the narrative from the verbal text and continue the story for some time. In *Where the Wild Things Are*, after Max declares 'let the wild rumpus start', the story is told through three double-page spread illustrations of the rumpus. It is no doubt highly significant that this wild activity is non-verbal. However it is not lacking in action and the illustrations depict this very vividly. Significantly, the words return as Max sends the Wild Things to bed — an echo of the opening image — and work in tandem with the pictures to illustrate the return to 'his very own room '.

Charles Keeping allows the illustrations to tell part of the story in *Through the Window*. Jörg Muller and Jörg Steiner use this device in a most sophisticated way in *The Bear Who Wanted to Stay a Bear*. Here the pictures appear at various stages as a series of frames depicting the process of the Bear's waking from his hibernation; as a double-page spread depicting the work in the factory; and finally as the stages in the story of his return to his cave. The illustrations also complement other parts of the verbal text.

Sometimes the words and pictures may seem to be working against each other to point out irony or to give a different perspective on an incident. The readers must hold these dual perspectives in their minds simultaneously. Michael Foreman's *War and Peas* seems to be a simple fable about two opposing countries in conflict. In the illustrations the most prominent features are the luxury foods that the rich country would not share with its neighbour. While the verbal text tells of the need for peace, the visual text acts as a criticism of conspicuous consumption. This deliberate counterpointing of the visual and verbal is used most effectively by Fred Gwynne in his books *A Chocolate Moose for Dinner* and *The King Who Rained*. While not truly narrative, these books provide a series of loosely linked statements made by an unnamed little girl of things her parents have said to her. Each one of the comments contains some sort of idiomatic phrase, that is represented literally within the illustration. For instance the comment, 'Daddy says he hates the arms race', is accompanied by a picture of dismembered arms running down a track.

Some picture books allow shifts to occur between the narrator in the verbal text and the narrator in the visual text. *Bear Hunt* by Anthony Browne makes these shifts. It begins with a simple, apparently third-person omniscient narrator, but this narrative perspective changes. Who says, 'Look out! Look out, Bear!'? This shift in narrative perspective is highlighted in the tense changes from past to present. The verbal text does not carry the whole story, in fact it reads rather like the text of a basal reader in its apparent simplicity. Yet there is something quite complex in the way the shifts of perspective work with the illustrations. In order to make sense of the verbal text it is necessary to 'read' the pictures. In doing so, readers enter into the joke that the writer is playing on the hunters, against this backdrop of stylised jungle. But even the jungle backdrop does not remain constant. The readers are given a number of perspectives on this: sometimes the stylised pictures are brightly coloured, hard line drawings; at other times they are devoid of colour as the Bear 'draws' himself out of each trap. The joke depends upon the readers' appreciation of the way Bear draws himself out of the dangerous situations into which he constantly falls.

The integration of words and pictures can be complexly interwoven. Where there is no narrator, or a narrator with a very low profile, readers need to work particularly hard in order to fill in the gaps and construct the story. In *Granpa* there is a very complex interrelationship between words and pictures that demands readers' full attention. There is no single narrator in this book. Rather, we have the dialogue between Granpa and his granddaughter. This is signalled by changes in the typesetting, as well as by other aspects of language. The dialogue does not comprise a connected whole without the pictures. These not only provide a setting for the dialogue, but also give some clues about the preceding actions or words which do not

Granpa by John Burningham.

When I was a boy we used to roll our wooden hoops down the street after school.

Were you once a baby as well, Granpa?

appear in the verbal text. The meaning of the opening words — 'There would not be room for all the little seeds to grow' — depends on the reading of the picture on the same page, as well as the picture on the following page. Readers have to determine that the line drawings on the left-hand page represent an 'other' time frame from that in the coloured pictures. In this case the picture represents an earlier time. Time is an important motif in this book. Considerable time passes in the story, and this is represented by the passing of the seasons in the illustrations. Other times, memories of the past, and hopes for the future are represented through the line drawings. Other references to time occur in the verbal text. It is impossible to read this text without a very careful reading of all the pictures.

Picture books of this style make considerable demands upon readers. The readers of these texts must be prepared to shift perspective between the words and the pictures and to be very observant of the details that the illustrations provide.

WORDLESS PICTURE BOOKS

Some artists would argue that these are the only pure form of picture book in that the entire meaning is contained within the pictures. Perhaps in one sense this is the case. The meaning may include an entire narrative expressed through a series of pictures. Readers must interact with the visual text to create their own internal thought narratives. Readers must 'read' the pictures, and this reading of the pictures may be translated into words in their minds, and may, of course, be shared with other 'readers'.

It is not strictly true to say that these wordless picture books are read totally from the pictures. The titles use text, and this does in some measure give a context or framework from which readers construct the pictures' meanings. Consider, for example a book such as Pamela Allen's *Watch Me*. In this apparently simple story a series of pictures documents the progress of the child who is trying out more and more daring tricks on the tricycle, until the inevitable fall concludes the story. Each picture in the series shows the child showing off to the reader, and quite clearly the child is saying on each occasion, 'Watch me!'. The reader constructs the meaning of this text by using the words of the title almost as a caption to each successive picture.

Words can also be incorporated within the pictures themselves and thus contribute to the meanings being constructed from them. This is the case with Charles Keeping's *River* — an extremely complex book despite its apparent simplicity. This visual text depicts the scene at a particular point in the river over a long period of time. Each successive double-page spread shows how the times have changed and reflects the values of a particular era. These changes with time are read in the pictures through the complex changes in the landscape, from idyllic countryside to developed modern cityscape, and through the changes in colours and hues within each picture.

River by Charles Keeping.

As readers turn the pages it is as if history were continuing in its relentless path, unable to stop for anyone. Within the sequence of pictures readers are able to detect words assigned to particular objects which further underline the changes that are occurring. Early in the sequence a statue bears the inscription 'Lady On Horse'. This appears a little later as 'O Glorious Brave', and finally reappears as 'Man on Horse'. In the early pictures there are few words ('Metropolitan Cattle Trough'), as we are dealing essentially with a pastoral setting. However, as time passes words become increasingly important and appear firstly as the names of companies who have moved into the waterside buildings ('Hirsh Brewery'), and as graffiti ('Dennis the Menace'); later as social commentary ('Save our Environment'); and finally as advertisements ('Win a holiday for two'). By maintaining the focus on a particular scene Keeping is able to comment on the changes which are inevitable with the passing of time.

Wordless picture books may also work through a series of pictures that move from place to place and allow readers to see a number of different perspectives. These wordless picture books very often adopt the format which we normally associate with the comic book, however they lack dialogue or picture captions: that is left for the readers to do. These picture books tend to rely on a series of frames with a single stage of action within each frame. The readers' job is to 'read' the image in each frame and to link it with the preceding frame and, arguably, to predict the successive moments in the action. The readers are assisted in this through the variation in the size and shape of the frames and their placement on the page according to the nature of the actions being depicted. Thus, where a series of actions in rapid succession is indicated, the frames will tend to be small and a number will appear on one page. Where the action is slower and perhaps more cumbersome, there is more likely to be only one frame on the page. There is an infinite variety of combinations within these extremes.

There are many picture books that fall into this category. All demand careful observation by their readers in order to fill in the gaps in the story. Shirley Hughes' story *Up and Up* tells the age-old tale of the desire to fly like the birds. The girl in this tale, after attempting to fly with a variety of disastrous results, eats a giant Easter egg and gets 'high' on that. The story of how she is finally rescued from her 'trip' through the air is told without words through a series of pictures which range from being tall and thin, to long and thin, to short, to whole-page, depending on the nature of the incident within the frame.

This is also true of Guillermo Mordillo's wordless picture books *Crazy Crazy* and *Crazy Cowboy*. Both these texts tell their comic tales without the use of words other than the titles. These books use vibrant colours and bizarre shapes to underline the caricature in the text. Sequences of frames are once again determined by the nature of the incident being depicted. Some frames spread across a double page, while other pages contain a number of frames. Mordillo does make use of words incorporated within the pictures in a way which serves further to underline the satiric nature of his messages. In the Wild West township in *Crazy Cowboy*, for instance, we encounter names on buildings such as 'Laurel and Hardy Liquor Dealers', 'Buster Keaton Barber', and in the city signs such as 'Strip Tease', 'Drive In', 'Drink', 'Smoke', and 'Blow Up'. Is it any wonder that the crazy cowboy decides to set off for the moon?

Satire is not the only way in which such frames have been used in wordless picture books. Jan Ormerod has used them to tell some very sensitive stories in her books *Moonlight* and *Sunshine*. Both these books focus on the story of a young child and her relationships with her parents at two crucial times of the day: waking up and going to sleep. Both stories are told entirely through framed pictures which once again vary in shape and size according to the action and events of the particular moment. The sequence of the little girl getting dressed in *Sunshine* is told in eighteen successive frames across a double-page spread and over another single page, each frame depicting a frozen moment in the process, from taking off her dressing gown to putting on her dress.

Wordless picture books make demands upon readers that are different from those of other texts. Readers must use the context clues that are contained within the pictures to construct the narrative. Readers need to observe closely the detail within the visual text. Very often the writer has provided assistance through the arrangement of the frames, or through the incorporation of words within the pictures themselves.

The Reader and the Text

VERBAL AND VISUAL TEXT

Many picture books are able to delight the young child as well as fascinate an adult reader because of their artistic completeness: the synchronisation of text and picture, the sequential and cumulative development of the story in text and illustration, and the imaginative originality of the story itself. Pamela Allen's *Who Sank The Boat?* achieves it with humour, Eric Carle's *The Very Hungry Caterpillar* with its novelty and surprise, while Maurice Sendak's *Where the Wild Things Are* achieves it through fantasy. Adults also can appreciate the artistry of such books.

There are other picture books which, while they may appeal to children at one level, are far more complex in the extent to which they require the reader to 'fill in the gaps' and, according to W. Iser, to become actively engaged with the text: 'To Iser, literature is not an object but an experience, and readers are not "consumers" but active performers who bring texts to life in their minds' (Thomson 1987, p. 112). In this context, there are many picture books that are more suitable for older readers' engagement with the text. Such picture books are more complex in the extent to which readers have to 'fill in the gaps', opening more possibilities for interpretation. Such a response to literature is investigated by Jack Thomson's 'Developmental Model of Reader-response', which is based on Wolfgang Iser's theory of readers as 'active performers who bring texts to life in their minds'. The emphasis in this model is on what happens when readers engage with the text. Here the concepts of 'implied reader' and 'implied author' are significant. As Thomson says, 'the implied reader is the kind of reader that the real reader is invited to become by the implied author, so as to participate in the production of the text's meaning'. Similarly, the implied author is 'the kind of person the text implies the author is' (Thomson 1987, p. 113). So the active process of reading is dependent on how the reader (or implied reader) interacts with the text.

This reading process is most interactive where a picture book is concerned, because of the integration of and interrelationship between

In winter he watched as she dozed by the fire.
All year round he kept her company.

'We are all right, John Brown,' said Rose.
'Just the two of us, you and me.'

John Brown, Rose and the Midnight Cat by Jenny Wagner.

words and pictures. A book that can have a powerful effect through this interaction is *John Brown, Rose and the Midnight Cat* by Jenny Wagner and Ron Brooks. While many young readers can react to the simplistic story-line of Rose and the two animals who claim her affection, there is a density created by the blending of the visual artistry with the text, and this density creates an emotional unease that is not necessarily resolved for readers.

Many emotional levels are aroused in readers of this book, with respect to the relationships of John Brown and Rose, or to the notion of death. The pictures in this book graphically symbolise the growing apart of John Brown and Rose as the Midnight Cat breaks into their relationship.

In 'reading' the visual text we are forced to question whether the Midnight Cat is in fact, a symbol or personification of death. The Midnight Cat seems to be coming to take Rose away from John Brown. Or perhaps the Midnight Cat represents the fascination with something else that intrudes on the relationship between Rose and John Brown.

Whatever meaning the writer intended, the harmony of the relationship is disturbed and the appeal of the Midnight Cat is definitely seductive for Rose. The Cat is described as having 'jumped up at the window and rubbed his back against the glass'. His eyes are described as being 'like lamps', and 'his fur shone against the ragged sky'. The Midnight Cat's influence is so strong that John Brown 'pulled the curtains shut'. In this episode the struggle is depicted in the emotional quality of the picture, as we see Rose kneeling on her chair to look at the window with her hands to her mouth in awe as she gasps, 'Look, John Brown . . . Isn't he beautiful?'

In contrast, we see John Brown's refusal depicted in the illustration as a clumsy attempt—the dog on hind legs, leaning, trying to shut the curtains, while the Midnight Cat is poised calmly between the two, on the outside of the window looking in. John Brown's refusal to acknowledge the existence of the Midnight Cat through much of the story is moving. Rose continually asks him to see the cat, but he says such things as: 'I don't see any cat'; 'There's nobody there'; or we are told, 'John Brown would not look'.

The Midnight Cat is frightening in his inevitable persistence, and John Brown pathetic in his jealousy and protectiveness of Rose. Do readers see the Midnight Cat as a threat to Rose or to John Brown? Several interpretations and responses are possible because of the multilayered meanings encapsulated in this overtly simple text. The story retains a 'universal' quality by the way it evokes in individual readers a sense of the fragility of human relationships and the finite nature of human life.

Through 'reading' the pictures, many of the above responses may be suggested to an individual reader. The front cover and first part of the book represent pictorially John Brown and Rose's relationship. John Brown and Rose do everything together: in the kitchen, feeding the ducks, and sitting under the pear tree. They are drawn physically close on the early pages—not only are they in the same picture on the same page, but Rose's dress and John Brown's fur seem to touch in the second and third illustrations. In the first, Rose has actually bent down and is reaching out, smiling to hold John Brown. The early pictures convey love and closeness between the two—their warmth is especially shown as they are cuddled up to each other on the fifth page.

On the first night that Rose is distracted by 'something' in the garden, the full double-page spread shows them separated for the first time: John Brown on one page and Rose on the other, but also turned away from each other—Rose with her back to John Brown as she looks out the window. John Brown has his head turned away from Rose and the window as he 'would not look'. The pictures really convey the emotional impact of the Midnight Cat's intrusion on their relationship.

Readers need to study the visual effects to respond to the layers of meaning that are embedded in this text. After the first separation of John Brown and Rose, for instance, the image of John Brown is dwarfed by the vastness of the nocturnal landscape outside the house. Yet the Midnight Cat is not to be seen here. The whole picture is symbolically shrouded in dark sombre colours. The car in the garage is, significantly, partially covered. In the next illustration there is a marked contrast. Here John Brown is drawn so large that he fills in one-and-a-half pages as he and the Midnight Cat confront one another.

The illustrator is conveying very strong messages about the interrelationships of all three characters here. For instance, Rose is missing from the illustration in which John Brown and the Cat confront each other. We see a very different picture of the positions of the characters in the double-page spread where Rose is putting out milk for the Midnight Cat. Here we are able to see, not only through John Brown's actions of tipping out the milk, but also through his expression, that he is aware of Rose's feelings and is uneasy about them.

Later, on the page where John Brown and Rose sit opposite each other and John Brown tells Rose, 'You don't need a cat. You've got me ', readers are made aware of Rose's feelings from her facial expression. In the background of all these moments of strong feeling between these two characters, readers become aware of the significance of the different photos of Rose's husband, which occur in different illustrations.

While *John Brown, Rose and the Midnight Cat* elicits this type of emotional response, Fulvio Testa's *Never Satisfied* evokes a humorous, ironic response through his use of dual narrative. Here readers are shown two different perspectives. The first, conveyed through the dialogue, is that of the two boys who are busy complaining about the boredom in their lives: 'It's so boring here! Nothing exciting ever happens', and 'Every day is the same. There's never anything going on'. The other perspective is shown to the reader through the illustrations. We see exciting, unusual, bizarre events happening around the boys who are so busy complaining they don't seem to notice them.

Anthony Browne's picture books encourage readers to 'share the game of the imagination'. The illustrations tease readers away from the text, in fact they often defy the text, directing readers into other fantasies that are sometimes in ironic contrast to the events in the text. Excellent examples of this occur in *Willy the Champ*, *Through the Magic Mirror*, and *Kirsty Knows Best*. Browne's work is often surreal. It has readers moving from reality to fantasy, from the present to the past and back, continually challenging, so that readers are encouraged to be actively engaged with the text: 'the reader's enjoyment begins when the text allows him to bring his own faculties into play' (Iser 1978).

In *Through the Magic Mirror* the child protagonist, Toby, is 'fed up' as 'nothing' is happening for him. Toby's boredom is reflected in the static, two-dimensional illustrations. The contrast is immediate when readers next turn the page and Toby walks through the mirror. Now readers have to actively interpret the surreal qualities of the illustrations as the 'magic mirror' takes readers out into the world where everything is crazy. Readers are actually invited to become engaged with the pictures as the text questions them: 'It seemed like the same old street, but was it?' Images tantalise: the window in the cut-off brick wall with the tail of the fish swimming past in one corner, and a head in a lower corner. Readers are led to be surprised in finding the unexpected: a tree growing on a concrete roof; an orange for a sun; half a rainbow between the road and a wall; steps that go nowhere. Further pages continue to tease: the invisible man; the 'painting of a painting of a painting; the dog taking a man for a walk; the 'flock of choir boys' flying in the sky; and the cat being 'chased by a gang of hungry mice'.

A continually changing perspective is presented in even more complexity in Annalena McAfee's *Kirsty Knows Best*, illustrated by Anthony Browne. Readers are led into a constant interplay between past and present, and between fantasy and reality. This study of an ordinary young girl, Kirsty, is presented with a maze of fantasies as Kirsty daydreams her way out of her unpleasant real life. The contrast is, of course, evident in the illustrations. The first contrast is of Kirsty imagining herself in an Elizabethan period as a carefree princess. This is compared with the real child in the dreary world of the twentieth century. The contrast is evident, both in the verbal and visual mediums. The clichéd verbal rhyme about how Princess Kirsty is planning 'the day ahead' is joking, mocking, tongue-in-cheek, almost from the point of view of an adult, as we see Kirsty reposing in a four-poster bed from another period. Yet this time change is contradictory in its period setting with the chamber pot under the bed and the alarm clock ticking on the bedside table.

The dull, dreary, predominantly yellow colours of the following two pages show the contrast of twentieth century reality, as does the switch back to prose. The voice of Kirsty's mother calling Kirsty to 'come down to breakfast or you'll be late for school', is described as 'shriller than an alarm clock'. Harsh reality is emphasised. The motif of the alarm clock is continued into a different time period in a different way. The lines of the illustrations are also harsh—the sharp features of Kirsty's mother reinforce reality further as she reminds Kirsty to 'stop

Kirsty Knows Best by Annaleena McAfee.

rincess Kirsty stirs in bed
And tries to plan the day ahead.
Should she rush to the Royal Stables?
Or help Cook lay the breakfast tables?
Should she joke with the Royal Fool?
Or call in at the Palace School?
Should she play with her favourite toys?
But, hark! What's that horrendous noise . . . ?

your daydreaming'. This is further emphasised with the real Kirsty now shown wearing glasses, unlike 'Princess Kirsty'.

The text proceeds through a series of contrasting pictures of fantasy and reality. When Kirsty daydreams it is of breakfast as 'party time' and this fantasy is paralleled by the total change from the real room's drab colours to the proliferation of party colours. A further contrast is in Kirsty's gloomy path to school, compared with Nora Nelson's ride in the Rolls Royce. Kirsty's next fantasy is in another place and involves a reversal of roles as the illustrations show Nora pulling Kirsty around in a rickshaw. The final fantasy is Kirsty's revenge on Nora who turns into a toad and explodes. The reader is left with the mocking comment, 'But Kirsty knows better . . .' with the suggestion that Kirsty really does know the difference between fantasy and reality—do we, the readers, know? Or *does* Kirsty know better?

The contrast of dull reality with fantasy is even carried over into the lives of Kirsty's mother and father, Mr and Mrs Little. First we see Joyce Little's dream of herself as a performer, 'Joyce Little, Superstar', while her father sees himself as a scientific inventor in a 'secret lab'.

There seems to be a whole area of response to literature possible in the reading of picture books like these so that they retain a dynamic potential for older readers across the range from adolescents to adults. It is particularly interesting to consider the way they can be read in the light of Jack Thomson's 'Developmental Model' of response to literature. Thomson's stages will now be considered concurrently with our analysis of the confluence of visual and verbal text.

STAGES OF READER-RESPONSE

Thomson (1987) has researched a 'Developmental Model of Reader-Response to Literature', based particularly on the reader-response theory of Iser (1978). According to Thomson's research into the reading response of secondary school students in Bathurst, New South Wales, there are six developmental stages that readers move through. These also can be identified by different degrees of intensity, sophistication of response, and reading strategies. The six stages of response identified by Thomson are shown in Fig. 1.

STAGE 1

Unreflective Interest in Action

At this stage, according to Thomson, the reader is not participating in the 'creation of textual meaning'. The reader sees characters as objects in the action 'playing out stereotyped roles', and reading enjoyment is gained from the action of the plot. Wish-fulfilment is part of the reader's response at this level: readers may identify with hero figures and action, but become bored easily because they are not

Fig. 1 Thomson's developmental model of reader-response (abridged)

Process Stages	Process Strategies
Stage 1 Unreflective interest in action	**a** Rudimentary mental images (stereotypes from film and television) **b** Predicting what might happen next in the short term
Stage 2 Empathising	**c** Mental images of affect **d** Expectations about characters
Stage 3 Analogising	**e** Drawing on the repertoire of personal experiences, making connections between characters and one's own life
Stage 4 Reflecting on the significance of events (theme) and behaviour (distanced evaluation of characters)	**f** Generating expectations about alternative possible long-term outcomes **g** Interrogating the text, filling in gaps, **h** Formulating puzzles, enigmas, accepting hermeneutic challenges
Stage 5 Reviewing the whole work as the author's creation	**i** Drawing on literary and cultural repertoires **j** Interrogating the text to match the author's representation with one's own **k** Recognition of implied author
Stage 6 Consciously considered relationship with the author, recognition of textual ideology, and understanding of self (identity theme) and of one's own reading process	**l** Recognition of implied reader in the text, and the relationship between implied reader and implied author **m** Reflexiveness, leading to understanding of textual ideology, personal identity and one's own reading process

'filling in gaps', questioning or 'generating expectations' about the text. Readers at this stage are not usually interested in the characters' emotions.

It is important to consider the reading development of young children at this stage, but also to see how this can be related to adolescents who may still be at this stage of reading response.

This is the stage at which young children usually read picture books, which is why books by authors such as Pamela Allen have so much appeal. Her books in particular require the reader to predict what will happen next, so readers are mainly concerned with the unravelling of events. Children want to read on to know 'who sank the boat' (in the book of the same name); if the Lion will return with the baby (*The Lion in the Night*); and whether Mr McGee will fall from the sky (*Mr McGee*). John Burningham's stories of Mr Gumpy have a similar appeal for readers at this stage. Other books that appeal to these readers, such as *Possum Magic*, *Two Monsters*, or *Felix and Alexander*, have more verbal text, yet are still more likely to be read for the unfolding of the events in the narrative rather than to encourage reading response on any other level.

It is at this level that a 'shared book experience' with picture books extends reading experience. The practice of the shared book experience has been encouraged for several years, particularly in infant classrooms, but also in other primary and secondary classes. It is a way of attempting to capture the intimacy of the bed-time story between parent and child at home, where reading is enjoyable and where the child and parent share their responses to the book through the reading.

A characteristic of many picture books is that the language is particularly suited to be read aloud and thus lends itself to the shared reading experience of parent-to-child or teacher-to-class. It is often a particular type of language that seems to combine oral language structures with the voice of a narrator that sounds like an all-knowing yet friendly adult (the omniscient narrator). Pamela Allen has said that when she writes her picture books she writes with the sense of the child on her knee. This is particularly evident in the language she uses which not only encourages the reader to predict ('Was it the pig as fat as butter . . .?'), but also encourages the reader to respond ('No it wasn't the pig as fat as butter').

Anthony Browne's books rely very much for their effect on the 'voice' of the narrator. For example, there seem to be two voices in *Bear Hunt*: the third-person narrator who tells the story in past tense, and the other voice that intrudes with comments in the present tense, such as 'Look out!' or 'Well done, Bear.' The colloquial tone in *Through the Magic Mirror* (Toby was 'fed up') creates the sense of the narrator talking to the readers. This is even more so in the sections where the narrator asks the readers to look at the pictures for answers: questions like 'But what was happening?' force the readers to read the pictures.

All this may seem appropriate for young children responding to picture books, but how do picture books fit into the reading of adolescents who may be at this stage of reading development? Won't they be the type of readers who may reject picture books? This is a possibility with any adolescents. Teachers can use this stage to foster interest in reading that will lead older readers into more advanced stages.

A shared reading with an older class using stories such as *The Man Who Wanted to Live Forever*, *The Moon's Revenge* or *A Piece of Straw*, would foster a class or group enjoyment of the unfolding of the events of the story that would appeal to readers of any age. The narrative structure of any one of these books can grip readers and in each case the voice of the narrator invites the reader to predict, question and respond.

STAGE 2

Empathising

Empathising means that readers are relating to characters in the story and feeling something of the emotions that these characters are experiencing. Thomson (1987, p. 193–4) argues that there are a range of empathic responses. He distinguishes the empathy that enables readers to have some emotional involvement with the characters, from the more developed empathy by which readers understand not only the characters' feelings, but also, to some extent, their own.

The process of empathising depends on the emotional development of the reader, the reading skills, and the nature of the text itself. Some texts invite readers to empathise more readily than others. Some individuals are more ready than others to empathise with the characters about whom they are reading. Some readers are more aware of the clues within the text that encourage empathy.

In conventional narrative texts it is the point of view of the narrator that directs the reader towards empathising with particular characters. The narrative perspective of the text determines the characters for whom we should feel sympathy, or anger or despair or condemnation. We do not condemn the hero and applaud the villain. The structure of the story itself, the actions, the descriptions of the characters, the incidents and events, and the point of view of the narrator work to structure the range of responses that we may make to characters in the story. Our own life experiences and the experience that we have of reading books interact with the text's structure to guide and direct our feelings. We cannot, unless we are psychopathic, applaud the actions of the wolf while condemning Goldilocks, or admire Snow White's Stepmother and reject the dwarts. Our feelings about the characters are circumscribed by the structure of the text itself.

This is even more complicated with the genre of picture books. Here it is not only the story told through words that influences the way the reader relates to characters, but also the clues that are embedded within the illustrations, and the ways in which the visual and verbal text are constructed. Indeed in wordless picture books the point of view of the narrative must be determined from the pictures themselves. In Jan Ormerod's *Moonlight*, for instance, our feelings are with the young girl as she prepares for bed. To assist the reader in establishing this, the title page highlights the girl with a single illustration of her holding her rag doll by the foot. We are immediately invited by the text to see the story from her perspective. As we follow her through the pre-bed ritual the pictures continue to assist us to feel with her, as she is continually positioned in the foreground. This is achieved by frames which act as close-ups on her. The text structure allows readers to feel the variety of emotions that the girl experiences in the process of going to bed.

In picture books that have both visual and verbal text, the point of view may be structured within both aspects of the text. For instance, in Russo's *Why Do Grown-ups Have All the Fun?*, the narrator gives us Hannah's viewpoint by relating what she is thinking and what she is saying. This is reinforced in the pictures as we see what Hannah is imagining. Moreover, we see some of the pictures from Hannah's perspective, as she peeks into the loungeroom to see what her parents are doing. The text ensures that we feel with her the emotions that she is experiencing before going to bed.

Readers may be invited to empathise with a particular point of view by being placed within the text through the direct use of the personal pronoun 'you'. The readers are firmly within the framework of the story as if they were present there with the narrator. This device ensures that the readers' feelings are directed where the narrator wants them. For instance in Alice and Martin Provensen's tale *Shaker Lane*, the narrative begins, 'Not so long ago, if you went down School House Road . . .'. This placing of readers within the text is continued as they are directed to follow the progress of the development of Shaker Lane through the accompanying pictures, with words such as 'Here is Old Man Van Sloop's house' and 'Here is Big Jake Van der Loon.' While readers may feel somewhat distanced by the life-style of the people in this story, the narrator ensures that the readers' sympathies are maintained for them throughout.

Readers may be invited to identify closely with a character in the story through the device of first-person narration. Once again readers are brought into a close relationship with the narrator as if the story were being told directly to them. Jeannie Baker uses this device in her book, *Where the Forest Meets the Sea*. The narrator in this story is a young boy recounting his experiences with his father.

First-person narration can be manipulated to enable the writer to tell a tale within a tale. This device can cause the readers' sympathies to shift between characters. In Chris Van Allsburg's *The Wreck of the Zephyr*, the narrative begins with a first-person account: 'Once, when travelling along the seashore, I stopped at a small fishing village.' There is a shift in perspective as the old man begins to tell the tale of the wrecked boat. Readers now join with the narrator in hearing the strange account of this boat. They tend to condemn the arrogance, conceit and deceit of the young man of the story and are inclined to feel that there is justice in the fact the 'the boy never amounted to much'.

The organisation, size, perspective and framing of the illustrations assist readers in adopting a stance in relation to the characters in the story. The perspective of the picture may reinforce the reader's feelings about the character. In Anthony Browne's *Gorilla*, the reader feels a sense of sympathy for Hannah whose father 'didn't have time' to take her to the zoo. The sense of her neglect is reinforced through the pictures which show the father absorbed in reading newspapers or working at his desk. These pictures are presented from a perspective behind Hannah, so that readers also experience the neglect and easily empathise with her.

Gorilla by Anthony Browne.

The framing of the pictures affects the ways in which we empathise with characters since the way in which pictures are framed changes the focus of the picture. Some pictures are precisely framed on the page; others have no defined frame outline; while in others the picture extrudes from the frame outline. In Innocenti's *Rose Blanche*, each picture is precisely framed. This works well to reinforce the ideas of imprisonment in Nazi Germany. The readers feel with the prisoners. To reinforce this further, Innocenti allows the barrel of a gun to extrude beyond the frame as if it is jumping out from the picture and threatening the readers. He also captures the flower and the barbed wire fence where Rose Blanche has died in a small frame, like a memorial picture on the last page to reinforce the readers' feelings about this young girl's sacrificial death.

Framing can become part of the picture itself with a frame within a frame. This can be further manipulated to ensure that readers identify with the key character's feelings about other characters. Charles Keeping achieves this in his book *Through the Window*. The scenes in this book depict the view that Jacob has from his window as he looks down on the street. Each picture is framed by the curtains hanging at the window. But these curtains are not static. They change shape from scene to scene almost as if Jacob is holding onto them and moving them in response to what he is seeing in the street below. Thus readers experience his view of what is happening in the street and feel with him.

The shape of the frames may also direct the readers' sympathies. In Munsch's story *The Paper Bag Princess*, all the pictures with the exception of the last are square, suggesting the binds that constrain the princess. When she has freed herself at the end, the shape of the picture changes, opening up into a semi-circular shape. The reader feels the elation with the princess that this shape evokes.

Colour is another factor which affects the way readers feel about characters in particular situations. Specific colours are associated with particular emotions. Charles Keeping effectively uses colour to highlight emotions. In *Railway Passage* he subtly manipulates shades of brown and a single contrasting colour to identify the particular characters who live in the houses in Railway Passage. These colours all come together on the page of cameo pictures of all the characters.

Uncle Meanie's sombre deep grey represents his dominant personality, contrasting markedly with Aunt Adelaide's peach colours and Aunt Emma's orange-gold.

Lack of colour can also affect the ways in which readers establish empathy within the story. Where an illustrator has chosen to use line drawing or black and white shading, the reader is directed towards empathy through the play of light and shade within the picture. In *Where the Buffaloes Begin*, for instance, Stephen Gammel has used pencil drawing to tell the story of Little Wolf and the stampeding Buffaloes. The black and white line drawings are shadowy and mystical, assisting readers to respond to the myth-like story.

Shadowy pictures allow readers the opportunity to recognise a mythical quality to the story. They indicate that this story is not to be taken at a literal level, but rather should be seen as a metaphor for some greater universal. Such illustrations point readers to identify with the character's experience of inner conflicts. In *The Fearsome Inn*, for instance, Nonny Hogrogian's illustrations, though using colour, have few hard-edged lines and tend to depict characters without backgrounds. The emphasis each time is on the emotions of the characters—fear, terror or joy. This supplements the highly poetic verbal text..Alan Lee's illustrations in *The Moon's Revenge* and *The Mirrorstone* have the same highly poetic quality, although they are clearly defined and very detailed water colour drawings.

At the other extreme of empathising there are books which appear to actively discourage readers from identifying with the character in a direct way. Instead of being encouraged to imagine themselves there with the character in the text, readers are made aware of the fact that this is a story and are distanced from feeling with the character. *Lizzy's Lion* by Dennis Lee uses alternating rhyming lines in a quatrain form which clearly indicates to the reader the satiric nature of this story. This story about the power we have over things when we can name them—particularly our fears—is told with the assistance of exaggerated cartoon-style drawings. Readers are not invited into the text to feel with Lizzy, but rather to stand outside it and to recognise the same feelings within themselves.

Cartoon formats and exaggerated drawings are a common device to assist readers to distance themselves from close identification with a particular character and to evaluate their own feelings about the issues raised in the story. Pat Hutchins achieves this in the story of *The Very Worst Monster*, a story about sibling rivalry. The readers are not encouraged to identify with Hazel because she is obviously an ugly monster. Anthony Browne achieves the same effect through his manipulation of the surrealistic style of painting in *The Visitors Who Came To Stay*. This story confronts the issue of step-parenting, an issue that poses some very deep problems. Brown's surreal illustrations allow the reader once again to step back from the issue and evaluate it without too close an involvement with a particular character.

Cartoons are an obvious method of distancing readers from an emotional involvement. The physical reality of the frames assists the readers in constantly keeping in mind that this is a story that has been constructed. They are able to feel the issues that the story raises from a distance. Posy Simmonds deals with the subject of death in the cartoon story of *Fred*. Raymond Briggs uses this device effectively to explore issues associated with nuclear war in *When The Wind Blows*, and to explore the injustice and horror of war in *The Tin-Pot Foreign General and the Old Iron Woman*. In this latter book Briggs uses quite gross illustrations of the General and the Iron Woman to ensure that readers do not feel any sympathy for them.

Now, this Tin-Pot Foreign General wanted to be Important. He wanted to do something Historical, so that his name would be printed in all the big History Books.

So, one day, he got all his soldiers and all his guns and he put them into boats. Then he sailed them over the sea to the sad little island.

The process of empathising in picture books is a complex one. While readers bring their own experience of life and books to their reading of each new book, they are also directed by the text itself as to where their feelings should be placed. In picture books it is not merely the voice of the narrator that evokes a response from readers: the illustrations also play an important part in guiding the readers' emotional responses.

The Tin-Pot Foreign General and the Old Iron Woman by Raymond Briggs.

STAGE 3

Analogising

In one sense the process of analogising is the obverse of the empathising process. Whereas in empathising with a character or situation readers bring their own experiences to bear on the structure of the text, in the process of analogising readers take their understandings of the text and apply them to analogous situations within their own lives. This process involves readers in making generalisations about the actions within the text and applying these to actions and events in their own lives.

Picture books offer readers the opportunity to learn about themselves and their society. They tend to do so by offering readers another or secondary world to enter. This may be a realistic world or it may rely upon mythical or satiric settings, mythical or animal characters and fantastic or magical deeds. There is ample scope for readers to find themselves within the text and to extrapolate the universals to apply to their own situations.

Anthropomorphised animal characters provide the reader with a distillation of human traits. Each animal may be identified as possessing particular traits which help readers to identify human types. In Michael Rosen's *A Cat and Mouse Story* readers are able to identify two basic types. The Cat represents the hypocritical bully who will use any strategy in order to achieve his own will, while the mice are shown to be gullible and accepting. However, within the story we see that the mice are able to solve the problem that this poses through co-operative and collaborative action.

Some illustrators assist readers to make analogies from the animal story to human experience through their illustrations. In *A Cat and Mouse Love Story*, the illustrator Michael Foreman includes within the pictures images of items associated with World War 1 — flags, military uniforms, medals and so on. Readers can then see very clearly the connections that the writer is implying and can apply these to other situations in their lives.

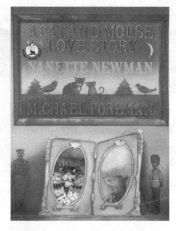

A Cat and Mouse Love Story
by Nanette Newman.

Picture books may offer readers a mythical prince or princess character who at first seems helpless or has a seemingly impossible task to overcome. This character may have to endure all kinds of frustration before being able to overcome the difficulties and emerge triumphant. This is the case in books such as *The White Cat* by Errol Le Cain, and *The Inch Boy* by Junko Morimoto. In the former the Youngest Prince survives the ridicule of the court through his love for the White Cat who turns back into the Princess after he has passed the test. Readers understand the notion of passing a test and can make analogies with their own lives.

Picture books also tackle difficult topics such as relationships, jealousy and death, allowing readers to apply what they learn to their own lives. In *John Brown, Rose and the Midnight Cat* we encounter all these elements as John Brown experiences jealousy of the Midnight Cat who is intruding on his relationship with Rose. The reality of old age is presented by Mem Fox and Julie Vivas in their sensitive book *Wilfrid Gordon McDonald Partridge*.

The retellings of old tales provides readers with the universal truths that are contained within all myths, legends and fairy tales, and which we have only recently re-acknowledged. In the retelling, the illustrator may in fact indicate the contemporary significance of the story. This is the case with the Anthony Browne version of *Hansel and Gretel*, with its modern setting. Alternatively the illustrator may choose to keep the timelessness of the setting so that readers must make the contemporary connections themselves. This is the case with a book such as *The Man Who Wanted To Live For Ever*. Reg Cartwright's pictures have a timelessness about them which reinforces the universality of this story. Selina Hastings' verbal text also has the simplicity and profundity of the myth: '"I am Death," he whispered. "And these are the shoes I have worn out running after you."'

Some traditional tales are retold with illustrations that set them very specifically within their culture. There have been a number of stories from Aboriginal mythology told in this way with illustrations painted in a style that draws on the traditions of Aboriginal art. Similarly the retelling by Gerald McDermott of *Arrow to the Sun* also draws on traditional Pueblo Indian artwork. This does not detract from the universality of the ideas. On the contrary, it enables readers to isolate the points of similarity because the differences are highlighted.

While picture books do not offer readers the same prolonged identification with a character as longer narrative fiction, what they do offer is a compressed moment in which the character—human, mythical, cartoon or animal—encounters some sort of moral dilemma that needs to be resolved, and in the process the character learns something. In *The Munros' New House* by Jonathan Gathorne-Hardy and Barbara Firth, the Munros learn that uncontrollable greed brings its own destruction. In Bob Graham's *Crusher is Coming*, Peter learns about the dishonesty of projecting false images of self. The child narrator of *I'll Take You To Mrs Cole* by Nigel Gray and Michael Foreman, learns the difference between fantasy and reality.

Sometimes the most important things that readers learn from picture books are not personal, but rather are about society. These could ultimately be lessons that are of supreme importance to the future of the world. For instance, from *Rose Blanche* we can learn so much about the effects of the Nazi regime that we should vow that such a situation must never again occur; from *The Bear Who Wanted To Stay a Bear* we are offered a multitude of lessons about the directions in which a modern technological society may go, and we should resolve to avoid such dehumanising situations; similarly, the lessons from *Where the Forest Meets the Sea* should stimulate us to consider the value of the world's remaining rainforest, and the value of adopting a conservation stance in relation to those parts of the environment that have thus far escaped development.

STAGE 4

Reflecting on the Significance of Events and Behaviour

At this stage readers are able to generalise about the significance of characters' actions and behaviour so that they can perceive themes, determine how issues may develop in books, and identify where authors are making comments on the human condition.

Many stories through the centuries have encouraged listeners or readers to reflect on the significance of the events portrayed. This response is particularly encouraged by the older didactic tales and fables. The picture book version of the La Fontaine fable *The Rich Man and the Shoemaker* is an example of how modern illustrators give their visual interpretation to an old tale. This new version of the story still encourages readers to reflect on the theme that riches in this world often bring anxiety rather than happiness.

The same theme is developed through Pamela Allen's picture book *Herbert and Harry*. This is a story of two brothers who do everything together until the discovery of a treasure divides them and they separate for life. In the author's comparison of the two as 'very old men' at the end of the story, readers are able to draw the conclusion that riches don't make human beings happy. Yet it is through the reading of the pictures as well as the text that readers are led to draw this conclusion. The second last page tells us that 'Harry had no treasure', yet the colourful drawing of him with his grandchildren on his knees shows us that Harry is a happy, peaceful man. On the other hand, the previous picture has shown us that Herbert still had his treasure but 'could not sleep', and we see the wasted life of a man who has spent all his years and energy endeavouring to protect his treasure.

It is in the reading of the pictures that these conclusions are drawn and it is through these pictures that readers are encouraged to reflect on the events. There is the obvious contrast between the early lives of the brothers who did everything together, and their lives after the treasure causes their separation. The early pictures show their happiness as they are pictured side by side either in the garden or fishing, looking and smiling at each other until the argument over who owns the treasure causes Herbert to push Harry into the sea. The contrast between the happy, early years and later years is shown in the change of colours. The peaceful pastels do not recur after the brothers are separated and only recur in the last two pages when Harry comes back into the story. There is a diminution in the colours so that they are fading as Harry, thrown into the sea by Herbert, is framed alone, swimming to safety. The major part of the story, which focuses on Herbert, is illustrated mainly in shades of brown and purple, suggesting the barrenness of the landscape and his life, as he 'takes the treasure high into the hills where no one would find it.'

As Herbert endeavours to keep his treasure secure, readers see him journeying further away from life and human contact, his fear isolating him. The infertility and purposelessness of his life is illustrated through the rocky, barren landscape, and readers see the burden the treasure has become:

> He walked many days and many nights.
> The land got emptier and emptier.
> And the treasure got heavier and heavier.

Even the 'highest mountain in the land' cannot give Herbert security. Readers see him growing older and wizened as he is shown chipping into rock, making a tunnel and a fortress to hide and guard his treasure, yet we are told he is never free from anxiety: 'But still, he can not sleep'. The final page shows Harry and his wife in the house that Herbert and Harry had lived in. The happiness is evident through the use of colour—particularly shades of green—and in the rounded hills. It is almost an identical illustration to that on the first page. The rounded hills, shown in Harry's happy environment are a contrast to the pointed, sharp and rugged environment where Herbert has chosen to live. The story of *Herbert and Harry* also allows readers to reflect on the sorts of conflict that can often cause deep rifts in families and friendships.

Junko Morimoto's books, with their Japanese context of setting and illustrative style, all lead readers to reflect on wider issues through the story. In *Kojuro and the Bears* we find that the theme of death is presented in an unusual way, but through the story it becomes inevitable that readers see death as part of the cycle of life. By the end of this story we find that 'the wheel has turned' and Kojuro has to face death, to become a victim like those he has hunted. Both *The Inch Boy* and *A Piece of Straw* demonstrate the triumph of the small, humble or poor over the powerful. Both stories suggest to readers that virtue will triumph over all, and a message of hope is conveyed. Morimoto's *My Hiroshima* is the most powerful of her books which shows from a real story the devastating effects of atomic warfare. It is the story of one small girl's survival of the bomb, and therefore a warning to the whole world of the danger of repeating such an event.

STAGE 5

Reviewing the Whole Work as the Author's Creation

At this stage, readers have developed an awareness of the individual writer's (or illustrator's) role in a work, and understand that the writer may be attempting to write for a particular purpose, to convey a theme, or to comment on an issue. Here readers begin to understand that a writer may have a definite point of view to communicate and readers' sense of 'implied author' develops at this stage.

Anthony Browne's picture books in particular encourage this level of response. His ironic, and often satiric, stance can be evident to readers through the author's tone and attitude. These are often conveyed through Browne's artistry as illustrator more than through the verbal text. The economy of his verbal text enhances the force of the visual text.

In *Piggybook*, Browne satirises the middle-class family through the tone of the verbal text as well as through the pictures. If readers are in doubt about his verbal tone, the pictures show his attitude as the husband and boys gradually take on the shadows and then the faces of pigs. This is where the pictures 'fill in the gaps' and help readers to attain the level of response (if they have not already reached it) at which they perceive the author's attitude and therefore can make fairly definite reactions to the message of the 'implied author'.

In *Piggybook* the attitude of the author is very clearly portrayed through the tone of statements such as:

> Mr. Piggott lived with his two sons, Simon and Patrick, in a nice house with a nice garden, and a nice car in the nice garden.

Piggybook by Anthony Browne.

The next day and the next night and the day after that, Mrs Piggott was still not there. Mr Piggott, Simon and Patrick tried to look after themselves.
They never washed the dishes. They never washed their clothes. Soon the house was like a pigsty.

"When is Mum coming home?" the boys squealed after another horrible meal.
"How should I know?" Mr Piggott grunted.
They all became more and more grumpy.

It is the repetition of phrases like 'nice' in the above context that suggest the author is critical of such niceness. This repetition also occurs when Mr Piggott's 'very important job' and the boys' 'very important school' are referred to. Yet it is the pictures that reinforce the author's disapproval. The nice house, and the very important job and school are shown through the pictures, and through the characters' dress to be very middle-class. The exaggerated poses of the husband and boys show that the author is making them the object of satire. A particularly clever example of how Browne does this through the illustrations is the scene showing the open mouths of the boys calling out orders to their mother in the second double-page spread. These open mouths become a motif which is carried through into the pictures of faces (even a gorilla!) in the newspaper that the father is reading.

In *Just Like Us* by H. Oram and D. Baird, readers are clearly shown that the author wishes to depict the way human beings are all the same despite the walls of prejudice or suspicion they may build between themselves and other people. Humour and exaggeration, achieved particularly through the pictures, show readers the author's attitude. The contradiction of Billy's mother, father, aunt and uncle alternatively accusing the people 'on the other side' of the wall of being 'very wicked' is shown by the caricatures of each of these people doing wicked things themselves. Whether the pictures are of the mother putting children in a laundry basket to keep them quiet, or the father producing poisonous chemicals, each of the characters is illustrated in a grotesque way: Billy's father with gas mask; his aunt with a large head like the trophies on the wall as she 'eats rabbits' hearts and sparrows' livers'. Through this visual exaggeration the author shows his attitude towards hypocrisy and prejudice. The narration of Billy meeting another Billy, who is a reflection of himself, shows that children do not have the same prejudice towards other people. Through this story readers would be given a very clear picture of the author's attitudes to certain issues.

Christobel Mattingley's *Rummage* also shows the author's attitude to issues such as social prejudice. In this case it is conveyed more through the language, although some use of caricature occurs in the illustrations. Readers see the author's criticism of characters through the use of language, particularly where verbs like 'snorted', 'sniffed' or 'barked' reinforce the visual caricatures of these people in the illustrations.

Thus an author's stance can be perceived by readers through a variety of techniques that writers use in their narrative and linguistic style. Attitude and tone are also carried through the visual medium to enhance and often extend that stance. The reading of a picture book can thus be a dynamic process.

STAGE 6

Consciously Considered Relationship with the Author, Recognition of Textual Ideology and Understanding of Self

It is at this level of reading response, where the more analytical and critical responses appear, that we would not expect picture books to appeal. Conventionally we might ask how picture books could have enough in them to appeal to this level of reader response. Surprisingly, there are many that do demand this level of response.

At this level, one reader may react quite differently from another to a book like Alan Baillie's *Drac and the Gremlin*. In this book there is an unusual attempt by the author to appeal to an 'implied reader' that real readers may be conscious of, but not really willing to become.

This book operates on a child's level of make-believe play. The verbal text and the illustrations support the merging of the real world of the neighbourhood garden and the fantasy world of gremlins, wizards, jungles and volcanoes. An interesting example of this blending of fantasy and reality is evident on the third double-page spread of the book, where the ordinary Australian suburban garden is identifiable in the double-page picture by the hose and sprinkler, the barbecue and the ferns and shrubs. Yet the haze (caused by the smoke of the barbecue) lends a mysterious quality to the child warriors. Readers can identify that the children have turned the real world into their fantasy world of play. The verbal text shows what these children are imagining:

> Drac fights off the Gremlin's treacherous attack with her ultra-laser beam.

> She chases him into the quivering jungles across the bubbling seas, and through the dark and poisonous fumes of the black volcano.

Drac and the Gremlin leap aboard her Anti-Gravity Solar-Powered Planet Hopper. They sweep through the clouds to the Mountain of the White Wizard.

Drac and the Gremlin by Alan Baillie.

Readers can see that a child playing can turn barbecue smoke and garden shrubs into volcanoes and jungle. Yet readers can also decide whether they wish to be caught up imaginatively with this game. Given the way the text develops, it seems possible for the reader to react in different ways. This is therefore very much the type of book which makes readers aware of the 'implied reader' the author is requiring them to become.

From the beginning the nature of the text operates to try to draw the reader into the game of the imagination with the opening lines:

> Shhh! Quiet . . .

and

> Drac the Warrior Queen of Tirrol Two, is in terrible danger.

The imperative nature of the language is demanding that readers take part in, and accept, the fantasy. Mature readers either accept the fantasy and go along with the imaginative game, or reject it and remain distanced from the imaginative involvement, while perceiving what the author requires of the readers.

Fantasy is often that area of fiction in which readers decide not to make the 'imaginative leap'. The language of this book could also cause rejection, as it appeals on different levels. While it seems to appeal to a young child in the illustrations (especially the close-up of the girl's face) and directions ('Shhh! Quiet . . .') the language is really pitched at advanced readers who need to understand the kind of terms used in science fiction or in medieval historical fiction. Gremlins and wizards are talked about, along with ultra-laser beams and anti-gravity and a solar-powered planet hopper. The level of language is at times difficult for young readers: 'She is fearless, as fast as the whirlwind, as wise as the White Wizard.' It is also the tone of the third person that shows readers what type of 'implied reader' the author is speaking to.

Margaret Meek referred recently to Shirley Brice Heath's research which shows that 'fantasy in texts for children is a social as well as a literary understanding' (Meek 1988, p. 18). In this light, *Drac and the Gremlin* could be difficult for readers because it is set in a middle-class Australian garden and it draws on the language of fantasy at a level that some children and adolescents may not understand.

Maurice Sendak's *Outside Over There* and *In The Night Kitchen* require similar responses from readers, although both books are quite different. In each book the readers must have a certain knowledge to make the connections and become the implied reader that the author is sharing his joke with (e.g. the cooks in the night kitchen are illustrated as Abbott and Costello). Burningham's *Granpa* requires readers to make different links as they read. In this case it is filling in the gaps in the verbal text. In a similar way the illustrations of Anthony Browne's *Hansel and Gretel* give a totally different and more contemporary interpretation of this traditional tale. Browne's *Gorilla* requires readers to draw their own conclusions about the ambivalent images of the father and the gorilla in the story. What is dream, and how much of this dream is wish-fulfilment? Readers at this level critically evaluate the story and decide what works and what does not.

APPLICATION

Thomson's model is helpful in that it shows the stage of reading a student may have reached and therefore also explains why individual students don't respond to particular texts. We are convinced that Thomson's model can show teachers how to teach the strategies needed for each particular stage of reading response, and that the use of picture books can both demonstrate and develop those strategies.

Considering picture books in the light of this model suggests how the same books can cater for the needs of different readers. For example, a reader at the first stage (*Unreflective interest in action*) would read *Willy the Champ* at the literal level to understand events and be wholly concerned with whether Willy triumphs over 'Buster Nose'. At the second stage (*Empathising with characters*), the reader may also understand Willy's embarrassment when he doesn't succeed at athletic events such as soccer or bike-riding, and be sympathetic for him when he is laughed at. The reader at the third stage (*Analogising and searching for self-identity*) would then consider how they are sometimes like Willy—unsuccessful. Conversely, they may begin to accept that some people can be different; that not everyone has to fit into a stereotyped mould.

At the fourth stage (*Reflecting on the significance of events and behaviour*), readers are more detached in their reading so as to be able to understand other people, or to fill in 'textual gaps'. In *Willy the Champ*, readers can be led at this stage to make value judgements about the implications of the illustrated contrasts between the more socially acceptable stereotyped footballers or swimmers and Willy who doesn't fit this mould.

Stage 5 (*Reviewing the whole work as the author's creation*) and Stage 6 (*Consciously considered relationship with the author, recognition of textual ideology, and understanding of self and one's own reading processes*) both suggest a more developed perception of the reader and the reader's awareness of the author's processes. In *Willy the Champ* the reader at Stage 5 or 6 consciously makes a judgement about how well the author is presenting the mock-heroic/ironic figure of Willy as a 'Champ', and how well the author is undermining the cultural stereotype of 'Champ'. Readers decide whether they agree with the author's satirising of the stereotype.

It should thus be evident that a picture book like *Willy the Champ* can be read at one or at all these levels by any age. The developmental stages of reading are not necessarily tied to age. The picture book is a medium with which a teacher can develop those later stages of reader-response, particularly with those 'reluctant' readers of novels. Readers can be led through a 'shared book' approach— whether on a teacher–class level or peer-group level—to enjoy the story, to feel with the characters, to respond to and evaluate the ideas, and to develop critical perceptions about the implied author in the picture book. The use of certain picture books can not only be applicable to particular stages but can help to move readers to other stages of reading response. In addition, the reading strategies and the understanding of narrative structure gained through such shared reading may allow readers to make a transference to other forms of narrative fiction.

Willy the Champ by Anthony Browne.

Willy ducked . . .

. . . then he stood up!

Shared Reading in the Classroom

In Part 1 we have identified and described a number of sub-genres of picture books, and have established how picture books can assist the development of readers, based on the research of Jack Thomson. We have also asserted that picture books are not intended solely for beginning readers (those readers who may only be interested in the story-line). The complexity of picture book texts draws readers far beyond this stage.

In Part 2 we present a variety of activities suitable for use in the classroom. These activities range from middle primary to upper secondary levels. The activities involve students in speaking, listening, reading and writing.

Underpinning all these activities is the belief that reading should at all times be an enjoyable activity. Sharing a text of any kind draws human beings together in their attempts to define the world and their place in it. We would not want to see the picture book become merely a textual study without the elements of sharing and enjoyment.

In sharing picture books with a class there are a number of possible scenarios. The teacher may read a book to the whole class, or to a small group; pairs of students, or individual students may read to the class or to groups; or there may be individual reading of the texts.

Whole-class sharing of picture books has been made even more attractive by the development of big books. These larger-than-life books make it possible for all members of the class to see the book clearly. We must, however, sound a note of warning. Not all picture books have lent themselves to presentation in this format. It is vital to be discriminating in making choices. Picture books which are to be shared by a whole class need to have a clear narrative voice, illustrations that carry part of the narrative, and situations with which readers can empathise and analogise. Big books such as Andrew and Janet McLean's *The Steam Train Crew* and *The River Boat Crew*, with their interactive text, delightful crosshatched illustrations and clear narrative voice with a gentle touch of irony, are ideal for whole-class sharing at any level. *The Paper Bag Princess* and *Great Grey Owl* are also useful. Other books which have not been released in big book format but which suit whole-class sharing include *Rose Blanche*, *The Bear Who Wanted to Stay a Bear*, *The Man Who Wanted to Live Forever*, *Never Satisfied*, *Through the Magic Mirror*, and *Aranea*. Obviously teachers will find many more.

The River Boat Crew by Janet and Andrew McLean.

The whole-class shared reading can be extended through use of Reader's Theatre techniques, depictions, improvisations, and imaginative recreations as well as a plethora of other writing activities.

Small-group sharing is an ideal way of reading picture books. Books that are to be shared in this way should have a density of visual text to draw the readers into discussion and interpretation. If the reading of the verbal text is to be shared, then books that have dialogue rather than a single narrator should be used. Books that have humour and irony are particularly useful here. *Winnie the Witch* by Korky Paul and Valerie Thomas and *Captain Teachum's Buried Treasure* by Korky Paul and Peter Carter are ideally suited to such a reading situation. Wordless picture books such as *The Enchanted Garden* by Susie Jenkin-Pearce and the Charles Keeping books, *Inter-City* and *River*, can also be very successfully used in this way.

Many picture books are more suited to being read by individuals or pairs. Many of the comic or cartoon-style books work well in this way. *Where the Wind Blows* and *The Tin-Pot Foreign General and the Old Iron Woman* by Raymond Briggs, as well as *Fred* by Posy Simmonds, and *Bill and Pete* by Tomie de Paola fall into this category. These books depend on readers being able to examine the cartoons closely. Wordless picture books and many of the longer illustrated picture books are suited to this type of reading situation.

The material that follows is organised into sections, each of which has a particular focus. It is not intended that teachers work slavishly through any section, but rather that they select and adapt the activities to suit what they are doing in the classrooms. Finally, it is most important to value and enjoy the experience of reading picture books and share this with students, who will in turn appreciate the shared reading experience.

Captain Teachum's Buried Treasure by Korky Paul and Peter Carter.

A Note about Availability

From time to time picture books do go out of print, but they do not necessarily stay out of print. When we began writing this book, *The Bear Who Wanted to Stay a Bear* was out of print. By the time we had finished writing it was once again available. If a book that we have mentioned is not immediately available in bookshops, do not hesitate to badger the publishers to reprint it. The books we have chosen are readily available in libraries. There are also many other valuable picture books available.

Words and Pictures

These introductory activities are designed:
- to awaken students' awareness of the potential of picture books to tell a good story and to make profound statements;
- to allow students to explore issues and concerns through an understanding of some of the ways in which visual and verbal texts work together.

The activities are not arranged in any particular order of difficulty. It is possible to begin at any point, or simply to extract some activities to use in conjunction with other units of work.

To complete these activities you will need copies of the following picture books:

- *Rosie's Walk*   Pat Hutchins
- *The Story of Chicken Licken*   Jan Ormerod
- *One Sunday*   Libby Gleeson & John Winch
- *Land of Dreams*   Michael Foreman
- *The Bear Who Wanted To Stay A Bear*   Jörg Muller & Jörg Steiner
- *When the Wind Blows*   Raymond Briggs
- *The Tin-Pot Foreign General and The Old Iron Woman*   Raymond Briggs
- *Granpa*   John Burningham
- *The Mysteries of Harris Burdick*   Chris Van Allsburg
- *The Wedding Ghost*   Leon Garfield & Charles Keeping

Rosie's Walk

▶ Tell the students that you are going to read them a simple story that is one whole sentence. Ask them to close their eyes. (Do not read from the book at this stage.)
▶ Ask the students to visualise the story, and to make quick sketches of the important scenes in the story. Allow time for the students to share the pictures they sketch.
▶ Read the words of the story to the students:
Rosie the hen went for a walk across the yard, around the pond, over the haycock, past the mill, through the fence, under the beehives, and got back in time for dinner.

- Tell the students that this story comes from a book which has twenty-seven pages, not including title pages. Give them a booklet with this number of (blank) pages and ask them to use this booklet to make a picture book telling the story of *Rosie's Walk*. It would be preferable to have students working in groups of three or four so that they can be engaged in plenty of discussion. Allow time for presentation of the completed story books and discussion of the choices that the students have made.
- Read *Rosie's Walk* to the students and discuss the way in which the dual narrative works.

The Story of Chicken Licken

- To prepare for this activity you will need to cover the bottom part of each page in the picture book.
- Tell students the story of Chicken Licken. Suggest that they might like to make a play from this story. Allow time to enact the story, and then to talk about what the audience was doing during the performance.
- Read Jan Ormerod's picture book version of Chicken Licken so that students can only see what is happening on the stage part of each picture. Stop at the second last page. Ask students to speculate on how the baby got on to the stage.
- Go back and read each page again. Ask students to speculate as to what might be happening in the audience each time. Remove covering papers as you proceed through the story. Read right to the end. Allow plenty of time to discuss the ways in which these two narratives work.
- Ask the students to devise their own story that involves a dual narrative—one story carried by the pictures, and another carried by the words. They will need to consider carefully where and how the two narratives intersect.

One Sunday

This book works on the same principles as *Rosie's Walk*, and could be approached in the same way.
- Give the students the verbal text on its own and ask them to illustrate this.

> One Sunday Dad and Amy drove to the dump. Dad unloaded a pile of boxes, a couple of chairs, and a broken fan. He threw away a stack of flowerpots, some plumber's pipe and the wheels off Amy's old stroller. Then they drove home for lunch.

- Show the students the front cover of the book and ask them to predict the nature of the dual narrative. Suggest that this should also have a humorous tone to it.
- Ask the students to construct a picture narrative that counterpoints with the verbal one. Allow plenty of time for sharing and discussion.

some plumber's pipe

One Sunday by Libby Gleeson and John Winch.

Land of Dreams

In this text the pictures do not tell a separate story, but rather they amplify the images of the narrative.

▶ Begin by asking students to think of some of their hopes and dreams—ones that may have come to fruition as well as ones that have not. Ask them to sketch these.

▶ Give students some of the words and phrases that Foreman uses for these: 'fragments of hopes and dreams', 'unfinished dreams', 'a scrapyard of dreams', 'the shape of a dream', and ask them to sketch these. Allow time to discuss.

▶ Read the story up to the point where the giant enters. Allow plenty of time to look closely at each of the pictures and discuss the kind of dream it has been and the type of person who might have had that dream. Discuss the sort of dream the giant might have.

▶ Invite the students to speculate on the outcome of the story. Be sure to encourage them to use the information gleaned from the pictures as well as the words.

▶ Read on to the point where the dream is launched. Ask the students to speculate on the ending.

▶ Read to the end and then discuss the ways in which the words and pictures have been used to tell this story. Why was the boy smiling?

The Bear Who Wanted to Stay a Bear

This is a very fine and powerful piece of writing, and in some ways is deserving of simply being read and shared. However it also stands up to many rereadings and promotes considerable discussion.

▶ Read the book to the class, but take care to ensure that all students can see the pictures, which take over from the narrator at several points.

The Bear Who Wanted to Stay a Bear by Jörg Muller and Jörg Steiner.

When they told him to shave, he shaved.

▶ In a second reading of this book, stop at those points and ask students to tell the pictures in words.
▶ Focus on the scenes in the offices. Ask the students to consider what they would need to add to the text in order to convey the messages of the pictures if the pictures were taken away.
▶ Focus on the size, shape and framing of the pictures. How could these ideas be conveyed through words? Could they be adequately conveyed through words?
▶ Read the story again inviting the students to consider which aspects of the text—visual and verbal—assist their own empathising with the bear.

When the Wind Blows

This is a very difficult text to share with the whole class because of the cartoon format. It works well if there are sufficient copies for small-group sharing.
▶ Point out that the first words of the text are 'Cheerio Jim', 'Cheerio', and then silence for four frames. Ask students to speculate on the significance of this.
▶ In reading this book, direct students to look at the powerful juxtaposition of the very small cartoon frames of the ordinary people, with the full-page spread of the war machinery, and the larger pictures of the warmongers.

Point out the narrator in the text who merely comments 'Meanwhile . . .'. Ask students to discuss the effects of this in relation to the size of the pictures that it generally introduces.
▶ Could this story be told in any other medium?

The Tin-Pot Foreign General and the Old Iron Woman

This is another book that contains a very powerful anti-war comment. Some people have expressed disapproval of this book because of the apparent anti-British perspective. It is not specifically anti any country, but is very powerfully anti the glorification of war and invasion and futile killings.

▶ Ask students to consider the comments that preface this book:

> Nationalism is an infantile disease.
> It is the measles of mankind.
> *Albert Einstein*

> Patriotism is the last refuge of a scoundrel.
> *Dr Johnson*

▶ Ask students to do one of the following:
  - write a piece of expository prose in response to one of these comments;
  - make a public speech using one of the comments as a topic; or
  - write an editorial using one of the comments as the headline.
▶ Collect some current cartoons from the daily press and discuss the satiric comment that is being made in them.
▶ Look at these cartoons from other wars. What criticisms are being made?
▶ Show students a picture of the British flag and discuss the significance of the red, white and blue crosses.
▶ Now read the book allowing plenty of time to discuss the exaggeration in both the visual and verbal text, the repeated patterns in both language codes, the use of colour, and the framing of the line drawings.
▶ Tell students that some librarians have refused to put this book in their library. Ask them to consider why this might be and whether such a stance is justified.

Granpa

This text works quite differently to those mentioned so far. There are enormous gaps that must be filled in by the reader using the clues from the visual text.

▶ Prepare the words of this book as a dialogue. Suggest to the students that it is the dialogue for a play with two characters. The rest of each scene must be presented visually. There are to be fourteen scenes in the play. All have one or both characters speaking, except the last scene in which there is silence. Ask the students to create a depiction for each of the scenes, e.g.

Scene 1

GRANDFATHER   There would not be room for all the little seeds to grow.

GRANDDAUGHTER   Do worms go to heaven?

The students will need to decide where this scene is set, and what each character is doing. They will also need to decide what happens in the last scene where there is silence.

Allow time for students to prepare and show their depictions, and to discuss the reasons for the choices that they made.

▶ Ask students to incorporate a flashback into each scene. The flashback has to be triggered off by something in the scene. It could have the same dialogue, or some new dialogue, or simply be enacted in silence.

Again allow time for preparation and for presentation and reflection upon the presentations.

▶ Now read *Granpa* allowing time for students to carefully examine each double-page spread. Pause before the last page and invite speculation as to what visual images will be there.

The Mysteries of Harris Burdick

This is an intriguing book. It consists of fourteen drawings each purporting to be a drawing from a story. Each drawing has a caption and a slice of narrative. There are limitless possibilities for exploring the stories behind these pictures.

▶ Give pairs of students the caption from each picture and ask them to write that story. Allow time for the partners to share their stories.

▶ Give the pairs the slice of narrative and ask them to construct the rest of the story. Compare this with the first version. Again allow time for the students to share their stories.

▶ Give the partners the pictures and ask them to construct that story.

▶ Compare the three stories that each has written.

▶ Now show the whole book to the class and have them speculate on the sort of character that Harris Burdick had been.

The Wedding Ghost

This is a very complex and deep story that has many echoes, not only through the literary allusions, but also through the drawings of Charles Keeping.

▶ Discuss the genre of the illustrated story book with the class and ask students to define what they think a few select pictures could add to a story.

▶ Select a few key illustrations from *The Wedding Ghost*. Ask the students to construct a story that these might accompany. Allow plenty of time for students to draft their stories, share them with other members of the class and discuss the reasons for the choices they have made.

▶ Read the story of *The Wedding Ghost* without showing the pictures. Ask students to select a few key moments and to sketch the illustrations that they would want to see here.

▶ Reread the story showing the pictures and allowing time to discuss the use of illustrations to amplify the imagery of the story.

Register

The term register has been the subject of much heated debate. The term is used here to refer to the sorts of choices that a writer or speaker makes in selecting language that is appropriate to the purpose, the context and the audience. At the superficial level this may mean that colloquialisms and slang expressions are not considered appropriate to situations and contexts such as public speaking and formal essay writing. But there are also important choices that are made by individual speakers and writers that are more subtle than this.

While it may be possible to 'teach' the aspects of register that are appropriate to a particular genre, it is far more effective to provide students with models of the different registers to read, and then to allow students to experiment with the sorts of choices available to them in similar contexts.

To complete these activities you will need copies of:
- *The Jolly Postman or Other People's Letters*
      Janet & Allan Ahlberg

You may also wish to use:
- *Each Peach Pear Plum*   Janet & Allan Ahlberg

The Jolly Postman

This book provides an ideal model of different registers. While it contains some examples of gentle satire, and depends upon readers understanding the allusions referred to in the text, it also provides a diversity of contexts, purposes and audiences within the framework of the narrative.

On one level it is a superficial text about the Jolly Postman who delivers a series of letters on his daily round. Woven into this simple narrative, and told through verse, are a variety of letters ranging from a birthday invitation to a letter of demand from a solicitor. Underlying all these is a wry humour.

In reading this narrative the students are provided with six very different genres of mail in addition to the narrative poem. Each one is presented in the form in which it would have been sent and is encased in an envelope within the book, so that students have the opportunity of examining not only the words, but also the conventions of layout that are appropriate to each genre.

As well as the opportunity for reading text written in a variety of genres, this book offers students a wealth of opportunities to explore writing situations.

The picture book can be presented to the class in a number of ways:

▶ If whole-class sharing of the book is the preferred method, it is a good idea for individual students to take turns to read each letter as it is opened. (Be sure to return the letters—they have a habit of going astray.) Before the reading, give students the roles of the receivers of the letters. To do this you need: Mr and Mrs Bear, Witch, Giant, Cinderella and the Prince, Grandma and Goldilocks. These characters can be strategically placed so that they can receive their letters.

▶ Small group sharing of this book is also effective. You will need eleven in a group if each student is to take a separate role. Again it is important to assign the roles in advance of the reading. It is possible to allow students to take several roles.

▶ Photocopy the reproducible activities on pages 53 to 54 and distribute copies to groups of students.

▶ Although many students will be familiar with the fairy tales which are alluded to in this picture book, it will be beneficial to remind the students of these stories. This will be particularly important if there are students from a non-English-speaking background for whom these tales may not be part of their early cultural experience.

▶ A useful text that can be used in conjunction with this is *Each Peach Pear Plum*.

The Jolly Postman
Janet & Allan Ahlberg

After you have read *The Jolly Postman* you might like to try some of these activities. Sometimes you will be asked to work in groups using improvisation or role-play. At other times you will be writing on your own. Be sure to go back to the book and reread the letters and the story to help you with these activities.

Activity 1

The first group that the Postman calls on is the Three Bears. He brings an invitation to a party at Goldilocks' house.

▶ **Group size:** 3
   Roles: Father Bear, Mother Bear, Baby Bear.
   Setting: The kitchen.
   Situation: The parents have to decide whether they will let Baby Bear go to the party.
   Follow up: Reply to the invitation.

Activity 2

The second letter is delivered to the Wicked Witch at the Gingerbread Cottage.

▶ Write the recipe for the gingerbread that the cottage is made from. You might need to consult a recipe book to see how recipes are written.

Activity 3

▶ **Group size:** Pairs
   Roles: The Witch and the salesperson at Hobgoblin Supplies.
   Setting: A phone call.
   Situation: The Witch enquiring about some of the products advertised in the pamphlet and the free Witch Watch.
   Follow up: Write the Witch's order form for Hobgoblin Supplies.

▶ Design a pamphlet for a series of products that you would want to sell.

▶ Write a set of instructions on how to make green tea.

Activity 4

The third letter is in fact a postcard from Jack that is delivered to the Giant.

▶ **Group size:** Pairs
   Roles: The Giant and his talking harp.
   Setting: The kitchen.
   Situation: The Giant reads the harp the letter.

▶ **Group size:** 3
   Roles: The Giant and the 'bloke' Jack saw who was bigger than the Giant.
   Setting: Mile High House
   Situation: Jack introduces the two 'giants'.

▶ Imagine that you are Jack and write the diary entries for your Magic Carpet Tour.

Activity 5

The Postman's next stop is at the Palace in Half Kingdom Road, where he delivers a letter and a little book.

▶ 'Fairy-Tale Princess' the headlines proclaimed. Write the story that would have followed that headline in the newspapers. You will need to read the little book very closely.

The Jolly Postman Janet & Allan Ahlberg

▶ **Group size:** 3
Roles: Cinderella, the Prince and the King.
Setting: The palace
Situation: After the honeymoon, they discuss the publication of the book.
Follow-up: Reply to the letter.

▶ **Group size:** 3
Roles: Stepmother, two Ugly Sisters.
Setting: The kitchen
Situation: Cinderella's family have just read the book that has been published.

▶ Design an advertisement for this book.

▶ Write a review of the book.

Activity 6

Next the Postman delivers a letter to Mr Wolf at Grandma's Cottage. The letter he delivers here is from a solicitor.

▶ **Group size:** Pairs
Roles: Mr Meeny and Miss Riding-Hood
Setting: Mr Meeny's office
Situation: Riding Hood engaging Mr Meeny's services.

▶ **Group size:** 4
Roles: Three Pigs and Mr Meeny
Setting: Mr Meeny's office
Situation: Three Pigs engaging Mr Meeny's services

▶ **Group size:** 7 (minimum)
Roles: Three Pigs, Mr Meeny, Judge, Wolf, his solicitor

Setting: Court
Situation: Three Pigs sue for damages.

▶ Imagine that you are the Wolf. Write a reply to the solicitor's letter.

Activity 7

The Postman's last call is to the house of Goldilocks. Here he brings a birthday card and a one pound note.

▶ Design a series of birthday cards for young children, for boys, for girls, for adults, etc. Write a verse for each one.

▶ Imagine that you are Goldilocks. Write the thank you letter to Mrs Bunting and her Baby for the card and the pound note.

▶ Look carefully at the picture of the birthday party in the book. Imagine that you are Goldilocks. Write thank you notes to all those who came to the party.

Follow-Up Activity

▶ Design your own 'Jolly Postman' story book. Select characters from:
- novels you have read
- famous people
- people from different countries
- animals
- people from TV shows
- rock stars

Narrative Sequencing

Some stories are told with a chronological sequence of events, and in others there may be considerable leaps in time both forwards, or backwards in the form of flashbacks. This section seeks to make students aware of narrative sequencing through the examination of four wordless picture books.

> To complete these activities you will need copies of the following picture books:
> - *Moonlight*   Jan Ormerod
> - *Sunshine*   Jan Ormerod
> - *River*   Charles Keeping
> - *Inter-City*   Charles Keeping

Moonlight by Jan Ormerod.

The Ormerod books tell the story of a family getting ready for bed and waking in the morning. The time passing is signalled through the size and framing of the pictures and through the different actions and events. The action moves from room to room in the house.

The Keeping books work differently. They require far greater cognitive development and wider experience of the world to fully comprehend their message. In these books, a greater span of time passes. In *Inter-City* the scene is the inside of a train—the Intercity—and this remains constant. However the view outside the train windows alters and it is this which signals the passing of time. In *River* a similar principle applies, although here the time span is much longer, and the setting remains the same. Within the single setting of the riverside scene much changes throughout the years. While there is no verbal text accompanying these stories Keeping does use words within the framework of his pictures.

In exploring the narrative sequence of these books there are a number of techniques that students can use. It is preferable to have several copies of the Ormerod books within the classroom and to have the students work in small groups.

Moonlight and Sunshine

▶ Issue each group of three or four students with one of the Ormerod books.

▶ Ask the students to look very carefully at the pictures, noting the detail in each and working out the story-line.

▶ Each group then tells its version of the story using words and referring to the individual pictures.

▶ Each group should go through the story again very carefully and caption each picture with a precise time. The caption could be done either on a separate piece of paper, or by using removable stick-on tags.

▶ Groups then report back to the class on the time frames that they see happening in the story. Allow plenty of time to discuss the reasons for the choices that groups have made. Particularly encourage discussion about the size and shape of frames, as well as the action that is occurring in them.

▶ Each group goes through the book again and this time considers what dialogue, if any, occurs in each frame. This can also be stuck onto the pictures using removable stickers.

▶ Groups then report back to the class on the dialogue they have included for the story. Allow time to discuss the appropriateness of register and tone.

▶ Ask each group to write this story using words and no pictures. Students should be encouraged to use whatever is appropriate from the dialogue they have devised. They will need to consider how much of the setting needs to be described in words since the pictures are no longer going to narrate that part of the story.

▶ Each group then reports back to the class with the results of its story. Compare these with the original visual story.

River

River by Charles Keeping.

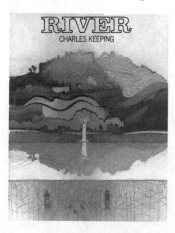

▶ Show the opening double page of *River*. Ask students to describe the scene in words. Notice the activities that are occurring, the dress of the people, the animals, the colour of the river and the riverbanks.

▶ Ask students to speculate on the date that this picture is depicting.

▶ Show the last double page of *River*. Ask students to describe the scene in words. Notice particularly the people, the activities, the colour, the riverbank, and the words.

▶ Ask students to speculate on the date that this picture is depicting.

▶ Divide students into pairs. Issue each pair with a copy of one of the double-page spreads of *River*. Ideally each pair should have a colour copy of a spread, as black and white photocopies are less effective. If this is not possible, students could hand-colour photocopies. Ask them to look closely at their picture and to write a detailed description of what they see in the picture and to speculate on the approximate date of the scene. Do not at this stage show the entire sequence to the students.

▶ Each group reports back on its scene. Allow plenty of time to discuss the scene, and encourage students to make comparisons and contrasts and to speculate about the causes of the changes they are observing.

▶ Arrange the scenes in the chronological order that the students have determined.

▶ Compare this sequencing with that of the book. Allow plenty of time for discussion, particularly where there have been differences.

▶ This book is called *River*. It is the story of the river. The setting is constant. It never moves from this spot on the river bank. Yet much happens as time passes. Ask students to write the story of the river. They will need to consider what the main idea about the river is.

Inter-City

▶ For this activity it is preferable to have multiple copies of *Inter-City*. Divide the class into one large and one small group who will deal with the narratives happening outside and inside the train, respectively.

▶ Issue each group with copies of the appropriate pages. For the group dealing with the inside story, this should also include the title page and the final page which show the passengers embarking and disembarking.

▶ Ideally the pages will be given to the students in random order. Ask each group to examine the pictures, discuss the contents and to put its set into a logical time sequence.

▶ Each group then reports back to the class explaining the reasons for the choices it has made. Allow plenty of time for discussion and encourage examination of the sequence and the cyclical nature of the narrative.

▶ Ask each group to write the narrative for its part of the story using a third-person omniscient narrator. Request that each stage be written on a separate sheet of paper. The best way to do this is to allocate particular pictures to particular people in the group. Allow sufficient time for the group to get together afterwards to collate the segments.

▶ Collect all the original pictures from the two groups in the order allocated by the group. As a whole class discuss how the two narratives could be incorporated into a single story. Arrange the pictures accordingly. Allow plenty of time for discussion and encourage questioning about the sequence and flow of events.

▶ Collect the written versions of the two narratives. As a whole class discuss how these two narratives could be incorporated into a single story. Arrange the pieces and read the story. Allow plenty of time for discussion and particularly encourage comparisons between the ways in which the picture story and the verbal story may differ.

▶ Read *Inter-City*. Consider the choices that the class made and the choices that Keeping made.

Moral Tales

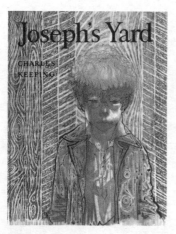

Much of the literature that we give to our students to study upholds the moral values that we consider to be important to all human beings. Sometimes these moral perspectives are presented in such a way that they are deliberately didactic. The view may be presented in the form of a fable. Very often in the process of the moral story the narrator intrudes to address the reader. In picture books of this type the intrusive narrator may be within the visual or the verbal text. This section includes a number of reproducible activity sheets which explore some of these 'moral tales' and the ways in which the morals are presented.

Joseph's Yard by Charles Keeping.

To complete these activities you will need copies of the following picture books:
- *The Boy Who Cried Wolf*   Tony Ross
- *Foxy Fables*   Tony Ross
- *Don't Get Burnt*   Jack Bedson & Peter Gouldthorpe
- *My Hiroshima*   Junko Morimoto
- *Father Sky and Mother Earth*   Kath Walker
- *Joseph's Yard*   Charles Keeping
- *Railway Passage*   Charles Keeping

Moral Tales

In this unit of work you are going to explore some ways in which writers and illustrators use literary forms to put forward moral views.

Activity 1

▶ Begin by writing down some moral statements. Moral statements are those that tell us what is right and wrong. Write down as many moral statements as you can think of that your parents or teachers often say to you.

▶ What sorts of things are you expected to do, or not to do if you behave according to these moral statements?

▶ Sometimes morals are expressed in the form of a proverb, for example:

- A stitch in time saves nine.
- A rolling stone gathers no moss.
- Too many cooks spoil the broth.
  What do you think these mean? Do you know any other proverbs?

Activity 2

▶ Divide into small groups. Select a proverb, and devise a short scene that illustrates the story of your proverb. Perform this for the rest of the class. Can they guess what the proverb is?

The Boy Who Cried Wolf and *Foxy Fables* Tony Ross

When moral statements are presented through a story we often call them fables. Aesop and La Fontaine were two very famous writers who recorded a large number of fables. Generally their characters were animals.

▶ Do you know the story of 'The Boy Who Cried Wolf'?

▶ What do you think is the moral of that story?

▶ Now read the version of the story retold by Tony Ross.

▶ What does 'c'est la vie' mean?

▶ What do you think is the moral of this version of the story?

▶ How would you describe the illustrations in this book?

▶ Why do you think Tony Ross chose to illustrate his moral fable like this?

▶ Read some more satires of fables in another book by Tony Ross entitled *Foxy Fables*.

▶ What makes these stories so amusing?

▶ What sorts of morals are they presenting?

▶ Select a fable that Ross has not used and try your hand at writing it in the same style as Ross.

R Don't Get Burnt

Jack Bedson & Peter Gouldthorpe

Sometimes writers use real human beings in real situations in order to teach a lesson. These stories are often called cautionary tales.

Activity 1

Suppose you were asked to write a cautionary tale about sunburn at the Australian beach. What sort of story would you tell?

▶ How would you illustrate such a story?

▶ Share your version of the tale with other members of the class.

Activity 2

▶ Now read *Don't Get Burnt*. Notice that the subtitle of this book is 'The Great Australian Day at the Beach'.

▶ Look closely at the way in which the illustrations work.

▶ Cover up the words on each page and read the pictures. Did you notice that the pictures tell the bulk of the story?

▶ Take each picture in sequence and write a different set of words to make a different moral. You might like to leave the last one out.

Activity 3

▶ In a small group, write your own cautionary tale. Choose a topic related to the environment—the Greenhouse effect, the ozone layer, pollution, or some other issue of national importance.

▶ Share your cautionary tale with other members of your class.

R My Hiroshima

Junko Morimoto

My Hiroshima is a very powerful story that warns the whole world of the dangers of another bomb such as the one that was dropped on Hiroshima in 1945. Junko Morimoto uses a variety of techniques to tell her cautionary tale.

▶ Read the words without looking at the pictures. Try to imagine what illustrations you would want to accompany such words.

▶ Now look closely at the way in which Morimoto has illustrated this tale. List the different styles of pictures. What effects do these have on the story?

▶ Look closely at the double-page spread of the bomb blast. Write a description of what is happening in the picture.

▶ Share your description with the class. Which is more powerful—the words or the pictures?

▶ Look closely at all the pictures again. How has she used colour?

Father Sky and Mother Earth R

PAGE

Kath Walker

Cautionary tales exist in every culture in the world and have been used to define what is right and what is wrong behaviour.

The Aboriginal people had many such tales in their culture. Many of these tales reinforced the closeness of human beings to the natural world, and the importance of looking after the natural world.

Not all Aboriginal tales are old. Many Aboriginal people today are still writing stories that tell a moral.

▶ Read *Father Sky and Mother Earth*.

▶ Notice that it begins, 'Once upon a world', and that these words are superimposed on the illustration. It also ends in the same way with the words, 'a new beginning'. In the middle of the book there is also the superimposition of words over pictures. Why do you think Kath Walker has done this?

▶ Look closely at all the pictures in the first half of the book up to page 24. Describe the things that Kath Walker has presented here. What shapes has she used? What colours predominate? What is she suggesting about this period?

▶ Now look at all the pictures in the next section of the book. Describe the way she represents human beings. What objects does she introduce in the story here? What shapes and colours has she used here? What is she suggesting about this period?

▶ What do you think is the moral of this book?

R
Joseph's Yard and *Railway Passage*
~Charles Keeping

▶ Colour is often a very important part of the symbolism of the cautionary tale. What colours do you associate with love, jealousy, poverty, grumbling, stinginess, happiness?

▶ Read *Joseph's Yard*. Notice how the illustrator, Charles Keeping, uses not only layers of colour, but also layers of lines in his drawings to suggest tone and mood.

▶ What do you think is the moral of this story?

▶ Look very closely at the last page of the story. Here the narrator leaves it up to the pictures to point out the moral of the story.

The reader has been very well prepared for this. Did you notice, earlier in the story, that the narrator steps into the story and comments to the reader on the moral perspective?

First his love and now his jealousy had killed the beautiful thing in the yard.

▶ Use that sentence, or make up one of your own, and construct your own story so that the narrator comments directly to the reader.

▶ Share your stories with the rest of the class.

▶ Now read *Railway Passage*.

▶ Look closely at the way in which Keeping uses colour to define the characteristics of the people in the railway passage. What sort of character is each one of the tenants of the passage? If you were to reset this story using animals as the characters, which animals would you choose for each of the characters?

▶ Notice the way the narrator comments on the story on the last page. What do you think is the moral of this story?

Poetic Language

One of the more difficult tasks that teachers of English face in the classroom is making students aware of and alive to the poetic qualities of language. This is becoming more difficult in a world where language is increasingly being used to express utilitarian and rationalist concepts. In attempting to waken students to the lyrical and sensuous qualities of the language we can utilise a variety of techniques. The picture books contained in this section offer students a number of ways of exploring language through visualisation processes.

To complete these activities you will need copies of the following picture books:

- *Wild Animals*   Brian Wildsmith
- *A Dark Tale*   Ruth Brown
- *The Wind Blew*   Pat Hutchins
- *Blue Gum Ark*   Jean Chapman & Sue O'Loughlin
- *Each Peach Pear Plum*   Janet & Allan Ahlberg
- *My Grandma Lived in Gooligulch*   Graeme Base
- *Great Grey Owl*   Orin Cochrane & Terry Gallagher

The activities suggested in this section could form a short unit of work, or could be extended into a longer unit with further poetic study involved. Individual activities could also be used within other units of work.

The focal points for activities in this section are:

- metaphorical phrases
- repeated patterns
- allusion and imagery
- stanza patterns

The books are used as models for the students to explore further the possibilities of language. Students should be encouraged to participate in shared reading, discussion, exploration and the construction of their own texts.

▶ Photocopy the reproducible activity sheets (pages 64 to 67) and distribute copies to groups of students.

R Repeated Patterns

One of the ways in which language is used powerfully is through repeated patterns. The writer sets up a pattern and repeats this with a number of variations.

▶ Read *A Dark Dark Tale*. Look closely at the patterns of words that are set up. Notice how the word 'dark' is repeated in every sentence.

▶ Look closely at the way the same word pattern has been repeated in each sentence. Make a list of the first word in each sentence.

▶ Now look closely at the pictures. What do you see in the pictures that is never mentioned in the words?

▶ Were you surprised by the last page?

▶ Look very closely at the page that says 'In the room was a dark dark cupboard'. What do you think will happen to the mouse?

▶ What do you think the title of this book means?

▶ Use this book as a model and either write you own dark dark tale, or make up a phrase of your own and write a similar style of story.

▶ Now read *Don't Forget the Bacon*. Notice how the rhythmic pattern of the words stays the same, but the sounds are different. Notice, too, the ways in which it is something that the character sees that triggers off the changes to the words.

▶ Use the following shopping list as a means of experimenting with the patterns, or devise your own list.
  • Five bread rolls
  • A bunch of carrots
  • A pound of mince
  • And don't forget the butter

How many variations can you think of? Draw the situations which cause you to think of these.

Another way in which patterns are formed is through rhyme. When two lines of poetry rhyme we call it a rhyming couplet. Writers often use rhyming couplets when they want to create a comic tone.

▶ The following lines are from a story that is titled *The Wind Blew*. Work in pairs and complete each of the missing lines by making it rhyme.

It took the umbrella from Mr White

_____

It snatched the balloon from little Priscilla

_____

And not content, it took a hat

_____

It whipped a kite into the air

_____

It grabbed a shirt left out to dry

_____

It plucked a hanky from a nose

_____

It lifted the wig from the judge's head

_____

It whirled the postman's letters up,

_____

Repeated Patterns

It blew so hard it quickly stole

_____

It pulled the new scarves from the twins

_____

It sent the newspapers fluttering round

_____

It mixed them up and threw them down

_____

▶ Share your versions with the rest of the class.

▶ How would you want this story to end?

▶ What sort of pictures would you want to accompany your story?

▶ Now read *The Wind Blew*. Notice how the pattern is repeated not only in the words but also in the pictures. Were you surprised by the ending?

Allusion and Imagery

Sometimes in setting up patterns, writers expect that you, the reader, will bring your knowledge of other language patterns to the text in order to make sense of it.

▶ Do you remember the story of Noah and his Ark?

▶ Do you also remember the song that begins, 'Old Noah, once he built an Ark'? The pattern that the song depends upon is a cumulative one: the animals went in one by one, two by two, three by three, and so on.

▶ Write a version of that song using Australian animals. Be sure to write it in rhyming couplets. Here is an example:
    The animals went in one by one
    Koala dawdled, too fat to run.

▶ Share your version with the rest of the class.

▶ Now read *Blue Gum Ark*. What patterns did you notice in the words and pictures here?

▶ In small groups, discuss whether you remember these characters:

- Tom Thumb
- Mother Hubbard
- Cinderella
- Three Bears
- Baby Bunting
- Bo-Peep
- Jack and Jill
- Wicked Witch
- Robin Hood

▶ What do you associate with each of these characters?

▶ Do you remember the game 'I spy . . .'? In your groups, play this game until everyone has had a turn.

▶ Now read *Each Peach Pear Plum*. Did you 'spy' all the characters? What patterns did you notice?

▶ Using this book as a model, devise your own game of literary 'I spy' using characters from books you have read. Be sure to keep the rhythmic pattern and the rhyme.

Stanza Patterns

Writers often extend the patterns beyond two lines, and repeat a rhythmic pattern over several lines. When the pattern is repeated over four lines it is called a quatrain.

▶ Read *My Grandma Lived in Gooligulch*. Notice the way the patterns are repeated here.

▶ Look closely at the way the story is told using quatrains. What patterns do you notice within the quatrains? Which lines rhyme? Which lines are indented?

▶ Look closely at the way the pictures are arranged. Notice how alternate pages have full-colour double-page spreads, and the intervening pages where the words are have no colour. In what ways do the colour pictures differ from those without colour?

▶ Work in pairs. Take one of the full-colour pictures and write a poem using quatrains that tells what is happening in that picture. Share your poem with the class. Compare your poem with the words in the book.

▶ Work in pairs. You will be given the picture of an owl. Each pair will have a different picture of the same owl. Write a quatrain for your picture. Share your quatrain with the class.

▶ Below is a list of verbs that could be applied to the owls in the pictures. Select the one that is most appropriate to your owl.
- wake
- glide
- listen
- swoop
- strike
- eat
- share
- sleep

▶ Write another quatrain that uses this verb.

▶ Below is a list of adjectives that could be applied to the owls in the pictures. Select the one that is most appropriate to your picture.
- mighty
- wise
- beautiful
- powerful
- deadly
- carnivorous
- kind

▶ Write another quatrain using this adjective. Share this with the rest of the class.

▶ Close your eyes and listen while your teacher reads *Great Grey Owl*. As you hear the verses can you imagine which picture is accompanying each verse?

▶ Now open your eyes and look at the pictures as your teacher reads the book again. Did you imagine the same pictures with each verse?

▶ In what ways did your verses differ from those in the book?

▶ What patterns did you notice in the words and in the pictures?

▶ Use *Great Grey Owl* as a model and construct your own book about an animal, using a similar verse structure and picture pattern.

Metaphorical Phrases

Words are a very powerful tool, and like any tool they can be honed to a fine precision. Like any tool, too, when they are blunt they are not particularly effective. In these activities we will explore a number of ways in which we can sharpen our awareness of ways in which words are used.

Naming groups

- A group of sheep is called a flock or mob.
- A group of cattle is called a herd.
- A group of geese is called a gaggle.

▶ What names are normally used for groups of: birds, dogs, horses, lions, elephants?

▶ Suppose you have been given the task of making up a whole series of new names for groups of animals.

What would you call groups of: politicians, rock singers, TV stars, police officers, teachers, girls, boys, disc jockeys, demonstrators, environ-mentalists?

What would you call groups of: reindeer, rhinoceros, bears, racoons, hippopotami, tigers, apes, lions, elephants, leopards, giraffes, kangaroos, foxes, otters, badgers, hedgehogs?

▶ Compare your lists with others in the class.

▶ Read Brian Wildsmith's book, *Wild Animals.*

▶ Compare your list with his names. In what ways are yours similar or dissimilar? Were there any words that you did not know? Did some of the phrases surprise you?

▶ Look closely at the pictures that accompany each of his phrases. What does each picture add to your understanding of the words?

▶ With the exception of the kangaroo, all these animals are not indigenous to Australia. Working in pairs, devise a set of wild animals of Australia pictures and captions modelled on Wildsmith's ideas.

Puns and Parody

BEAR HUNT
Anthony Browne

Bear Hunt by Anthony Browne.

Puns involve a humorous play with words so that differing meanings of a word or words are highlighted. Parody involves the humorous imitation of a serious literary or artistic work, often with a satirical intent. The parody uses a variety of devices to achieve its effect. Hyperbole, or exaggeration, is one of the main features, and puns very often play a role.

> To complete these activities you will need copies of:
> ■ *Bear Hunt*   Anthony Browne

In order to understand the ways in which parody works, we need to know something of the format of the original literary or artistic work and to be able to retain this in our perception as we interact with the parodied form. Similarly, in responding to puns we must also retain the often paradoxical meanings of the same word at one and the same time.

Bear Hunt allows the opportunity to explore this as it is a parody that also involves a visual pun. On the surface it seems to be a very slight text, merely a picture/caption book. However it goes far beyond this, since it parodies the basal readers that so many of our students were subjected to in their early reading experiences. Students immediately remember and recognise the form. As they explore the pun and the visual text, they are able to use the satirical commentary, and are transported to an almost surrealistic realm.

There are a variety of ways of introducing this book to a class. Because of the detail of the visual text it is better if shared in small groups. It is also advisable to engage students in discussion of their early memories of learning to read. They will probably recall the text of some of their basal readers. It may even be worthwhile examining one or two of these now-outmoded 'books' prior to the reading of the text. One of the issues that is raised by *Bear Hunt* is the question of just what happens in our heads when we read. Many students who have been taught to read through the phonic method, using the structured basal readers, believe that all the meaning is in the text: that readers are not expected to bring anything to the text, but merely extract information from it. *Bear Hunt* explodes this myth and will stimulate a great deal of discussion in the process.

The approach here is to have the students explore the alternate meanings that are possible both for the pictures and for the words and then to experience the book itself, holding the alternate possibilities in their minds.

▶ For students to complete the reproducible activities on pages 69 to 70, you will need to cover the text that accompanies the first two illustrations in *Bear Hunt*.

Bear Hunt

Anthony Browne

- Do you remember how you first learned to read? Get together in small groups and share your memories.
  - What features do you have in common?
  - What is the first book you remember reading?
  - How did you work out what words meant?
  - What part did pictures play in the process?

- Working with a partner, imagine that you have been asked by the editor of a dictionary to write a succinct definition of the terms 'read' and 'reading'. Write the definition that you would want included in the dictionary.

- Compare your definitions with those of the rest of the class. What features do they have in common? In what ways do they differ?

- These words come from a book that is like the ones many of you would have used to learn to read. Such books are called 'basal readers'.

  One day Bear went for a walk.
  Two Hunters were hunting.
  They saw Bear
  Look out! Look out, Bear!
  Quickly Bear began to draw.
  Well done, Bear.
  But there was another Hunter.
  Run, Bear, Run.
  Out came Bear's pencil.
  And Bear walked on.
  Stop, the Hunter's back . . .
  Swiftly Bear got to work.
  Look up Bear!

  Bear is caught.
  But Bear still had his pencil . . .
  Clever Bear!
  Help!
  Do something Bear!
  So Bear escaped . . .
  . . . and the Hunters were left far, far behind.

- Imagine that your group has been asked by the publisher to devise the pictures for this story. Using drawings, photographs or graphics on a computer, devise the pictures that you think should go with these words.

- What sorts of choices did you make in devising the pictures to go with this 'story'?

- What implement did you give Bear to 'draw' with?

- Look up the word 'draw' in a dictionary. Notice how many meanings the word has. What other words do you know that have multiple meanings?

- Now let's meet Anthony Browne's Bear and Hunters. (Your teacher should now show you the first two pictures in *Bear Hunt* without the words.)

- Look closely at these two pictures. Is this how you visualised the Bear and the Hunters?

- Write a description of the Bear. What is the weapon that he uses to 'draw' with?

- Write a description of the jungle that Bear is walking through. Look very closely at the flowers and the leaves and the creature lurking in the undergrowth. This serpent-like creature has a special pattern

Bear Hunt Anthony Browne

on its skin. It is a harlequin pattern. Harlequin was originally a very droll character from pantomime who wore parti-coloured tights in this pattern. He usually carried a magic wand that enabled him to get out of trouble.

▶ Write a description of the Hunters. Describe the vehicle they are travelling in. Look closely at the front of the car, the side door and at the wheels. Look closely at the background. Notice the animal hiding.

▶ These are the first two pictures in *Bear Hunt*. What do you now expect the rest of the pictures will be?

▶ Now read the rest of the book together. This will be better if you have several copies so that you can read it in small groups.

▶ Now go back and examine each page. Look closely at the page that has the caption 'They saw Bear'.
  • Where are the Hunters?
  • In what ways has the jungle changed?
  • Look closely at the leaves.
  • What effects do these pictures have on the meanings of the words?

▶ Examine the page that says 'Look out! Look out Bear!'.
  • What implement is the Hunter using?
  • What would you normally expect to catch with this?
  • How has the jungle changed?
  • List all the items that are incorporated in the jungle background that seem to be out of place.

▶ Look at the page that says 'Quickly Bear began to draw'.
  • Which meaning of 'draw' would you expect in such a situation?
  • If you did not have the picture, would you expect that Bear might draw a gun? Anthony Browne is playing with the meanings of the words here.

▶ Look closely at the next page.
  • What has Bear drawn?
  • What has changed now in the jungle background?

▶ Look at the page that says 'But there was another Hunter'.
  • What weapon is this Hunter using?
  • What would you normally expect to catch with this?
  • Examine the jungle background carefully. What changes have been made now?

▶ Look at the page that says 'Run, Bear, Run!' What do you see in the jungle now?

▶ Look closely at each page as the Hunters attempt to catch Bear.
  • What happens to the jungle background?
  • What weapoons do the hunters use?
  • Are they appropriate for catching bears?
  • What is the effect of the intense colour in the jungle and the whiteness of Bear and the Dove and Rhinoceros?

▶ Is this a serious basal reader?

▶ Try to find one of the basal readers that you used when you were first learning to read. Devise a parody of the book using some of the ideas that Browne has employed.

Satire

Satire is often a difficult concept for students to understand. In order to do so they need to hold differing and often contrary perspectives on a topic at one time. They need to understand that, while the satirist uses ridicule and humour, a serious point is being made. The tools of the satirist include exaggeration, inversion and incongruity. There are many picture books that make this obvious to the reader and are useful in showing students how the devices of satire work.

The Paper Bag Princess by Robert N. Munsch.

> To complete these activities you will need copies of the following picture books:
> - *Crazy Crazy*   Guillermo Mordillo
> - *Piggybook*   Anthony Browne
> - *The Paper Bag Princess*   Robert Munsch & Michael Martchenko
> - *Princess Smartypants*   Babette Cole
> - *Prince Cinders*   Babette Cole
> - *Willy the Champ*   Anthony Browne
> - *Willy the Wimp*   Anthony Browne
> - *War and Peas*   Michael Foreman
> - *The Tin-Pot Foreign General and the Old Iron Woman*   Raymond Briggs

Crazy Crazy

This is a wordless picture book with cartoon-style illustrations. It depends for its effects upon gross exaggeration of colour, line, situation and characters.

- ▶ Ask students to describe what life in a jungle might be like. Be sure to encourage realistic descriptions that encompass both the beauty and the terror.
- ▶ Ask students to speculate on what might happen to an unarmed man who ventured barefoot and scantily clad into such a jungle.
- ▶ Ask students to speculate on how a cartoon film might represent this scenario.
- ▶ Read *Crazy Crazy*. This is best done in small groups so that there are plenty of opportunities for all students to examine the illustrations close up.
- ▶ Ask students to list all the incongruous activities in the book.
- ▶ Ask them to speculate on what the author is satirising in a light-hearted and humorous way.

Piggybook

▶ Photocopy the reproducible activity sheet and distribute copies to groups of students.

The Paper Bag Princess

This book can be used in its big book form, or in the small version.
▶ Begin by asking students to retell the fairy tale story of the princess who is rescued by the prince from the dangerous and fiery dragon.
▶ Ask students to identify the stereotypes which have emerged from that type of story.
▶ Show students the first page of *The Paper Bag Princess* and read the words. Ask the students to predict what might happen in this story if it were a traditional tale. Ask them to identify any features of the illustrations or the words that suggest that this story will not proceed in the traditional manner.
▶ Read the next page. Ask students to identify the inversion that has occurred and to predict what will happen as a result.
▶ Read on to the point where Elizabeth arrives at the cave. Ask students to identify what is incongruous here.
▶ Read on to the point where the dragon is 'so tired he didn't even move'. Ask students to identify the inversions here. What female wiles has Elizabeth employed? Ask students to predict how this story will end.
▶ Read the next page. Ask students to write Elizabeth's reply and to sketch the illustration that they think should highlight this. Remind them that the story has so far inverted the traditional tale and used a variety of incongruous elements to do this.
▶ Allow time for the students to share their endings with the rest of the class.
▶ Read the final page. Compare Munsch's version with those that the students have written. In what ways are they similar and in what ways do they differ?

Princess Smartypants

▶ Recall with students the fairy tales about princesses, toads, and princes who must complete deeds in order to win the princesses' hands in marriage. Discuss with the students the ideas that these tales highlight.
▶ Ask students to write a description of a princess on one half of a sheet of paper. On the other half, ask them to write a parallel description of a princess who is called 'Smartypants'. They will need to invert and exaggerate the first piece to achieve this.
▶ Show students the title page of *Princess Smartypants* and ask them to speculate on the events of this book.
▶ Read the book through to where Prince Swashbuckle arrives, allowing time for students to notice the incongruous images in both

the words and the illustrations, for instance the way the visual images of her pets are at odds with the normal connotations of the word. Encourage discussion of the ways in which exaggeration has been used. Ask students to comment on the names of the Princes and the way these are further exaggerated through the visual images.

▶ Ask students to predict the remainder of the story. What features of the words and pictures suggest this kind of ending?

▶ Read on to the page where she gives the Prince the magic kiss. Encourage students to discuss the ways in which the illustrations have altered, and the changes that have occurred in the verbal text. Ask them to predict the ending now. What features of the text suggest this ending? Does it differ from the students' earlier predictions?

▶ Read to the end and allow time to discuss the ways in which the traditional tales have been distorted.

War and Peas

This is an interesting little book that depends very much on the pun in the title phrase, and the subsequent visual puns on phrases such as 'supply trucks'.

▶ Read the words of the story to the students without showing them the title or the pictures. Ask the students to describe the scene that they have imagined as they listened to the story.

▶ Tell the students that this story is in fact a satire and that the satire is presented through the illustrations. Ask them to sketch satiric illustrations for these phrases:

- the hills of the neighbouring kingdom
- the richness of everything
- the main square
- the entire fat army

Suddenly the Lion and the Grocer were seized by guards and taken to the main square.

War and Peas by Michael Foreman.

- trucks full of supplies
- the supply trucks
- hundreds of seeds

▶ Allow time for sharing and discussion of the images that students have developed.

▶ Read *War and Peas* showing the pictures and discussing the ways in which the exaggeration and incongruity work to point out the satire.

The Tin-Pot Foreign General and the Old Iron Woman

This is a very savage satire on war and the glorification of victory.

▶ Encourage students to discuss their own views of war and to explore the differing views that are held by different cultures and in different epochs.

▶ This book rewards close study and frequent rereading. Encourage students to discuss ways in which the juxtaposition of the cartoon images and the sombre line drawings work to point out the bitterness of the satire.

Prince Cinders

▶ Ask students to recall the story of Cinderella. Identify the stereotypes and ideas that occur in that tale.

▶ Ask students to retell the tale from a different perspective, setting it in a modern or future time and place, and making the key character of Cinderella male.

▶ Allow time for the students to share their versions of the story.

▶ Read *Prince Cinders*, allowing time to discuss the ways in which the traditional tale is being ridiculed through both the pictures and the words.

Willy the Champ and Willy the Wimp

These two tales further satirise stereotypical images of males as strong and aggressive.

▶ Ask students to define and describe the 'perfect male' and the 'perfect female'. Discuss the characteristics that they have nominated.

▶ Ask students to identify the words that are used to perjoratively describe someone who does not fit into the designated categories.

▶ Ask students to identify the connotations they have for the words 'champ' and 'wimp'.

▶ Read the two Willy books encouraging students to discuss how the stereotypes are set up and then ridiculed through the words and the pictures. Notice how few words there are in these texts and how much of the satire is carried through the pictures.

▶ Ask the students to identify the ideas that Browne is satirising.

This book makes some very strong satiric statements through both the visual and the verbal text. You are going to explore some of the things that the author, Anthony Browne, is criticising.

▶ Work in small groups. Each group should be allocated one of the following categories: men, women, boys. In your group, draw up a profile of the perfect role for the category that you have been allocated.

▶ In pairs, write a description of a pig.
- What is usually meant when this term is used perjoratively?
- What do you mean if you call a human being a pig?

▶ Working with a partner, write down what you understand by the term 'piggyback'. Who would you give a piggyback to? Who would you want to give you a piggyback?

▶ Now your teacher will show you the cover of the book by Anthony Browne called *Piggybook*. Discuss what you see on the front cover of this book. Who is giving the piggyback?

▶ Why do you think the book is called *Piggybook*? What do you think this book will be about? Do you think it will be a serious book? Why?

▶ Now look at the title page and the dedication page of this book. Why do you think there are flying pigs on this page? Have you heard of the saying 'Pigs might fly!'? What do you think it means?

▶ Read the first page of the story. Look very closely at the photograph. What is suggested by the pose of the three males in this picture? Where is Mr Piggott's wife?

▶ Look closely at the words. What do you think is meant by the word 'nice'? What is the implication of the word 'inside'?

▶ What do you think this book will be about?

▶ Read the next page. Look closely at the open mouths. What does this remind you of?

▶ Read the next double page. What images of the mother appear on this double-page spread? What effect does the change of colour have? What change of tone is evident in the words?

▶ Read the next page. What is the effect of the shadow on the wall? Look closely at Mr Piggott's buttonhole. What do you think will occur next?

▶ Look closely at the next two pages. Why do you think Anthony Browne has framed the face of Mr Piggott eating the sausage in this way? What kind of sausage do you think he is eating?

▶ Look closely at the next double-page spread. Make a list of the images of pigs that are evident here.

▶ Read through the next pages looking very closely at the pictures, and listing all the images of pigs that you find. Look closely at the wallpaper, the door handles, the light switches, the moon, the tea pot and so on.

Aboriginal Stories

Pigs and Honey by Jeanie Adams.

To complete these activities you will need copies of the following picture books:

- *The Quinkins*   Percy Trezise & Dick Roughsey
- *This is Still Rainbow Snake Country*   Catherine Berndt illustrated by Raymond Meek
- *The Peopling of Australia*   Percy Trezise
- *Pigs and Honey*   Jeanie Adams

From the beginning of time, story has been central to the preservation and transmission of culture. It contains all that is precious to a people: religion, history, science, philosophy and education. Nowhere is the centrality of story more evident than in the Aboriginal stories of the Dreamtime. Stories can therefore provide a way into a culture which is still full of unexplained mysteries.

The few picture books which tell Aboriginal stories are almost all told from a white Eurocentric world view. Firstly, they are mostly told in standard English. Though each of the several hundred Aboriginal nations has a distinct language, few survive intact. The various dialects of Aboriginal English appear in published stories only in occasional phrases, to give 'colour' and atmosphere. Secondly, most authors attempt to preserve the oral tradition of the Dreamtime stories by borrowing from a Western tradition using slightly archaic English words. Thirdly, most stories have a shape that conforms to European notions of narrative structure.

In this sense, these books are not examples of how a community creates story to reflect itself. Rather, they are attempts at creating a bridge between two cultures, and at explaining or interpreting Aboriginal stories for others. This is how *The Quinkins*, by Percy Trezise and Dick Roughsey, begins:

> From the beginning the Yalanji tribe belonged to the beautiful country of Cape York. They covered the walls of open caves with their paintings of ancestral beings, sacred animals — and the Quinkins.

There is an interesting contrast between this opening, which gives the reader time, space and character markers with which they are familiar, and the beginning of the next story which is an attempt by

The Imjim were small, fat-bellied, bad fellows, with large ugly heads, long teeth and claws. They stole children and took them to their cave in the great red mountain called Boonbalbee. The Imjim had long, knobbly tails that they used like a kangaroo to travel in giant leaps across the land.

Timara was the name of the other Quinkins. They were humorous, whimsical spirits who liked to play tricks on people, but they didn't like the Imjim stealing children and always tried to stop them. The Timara were very tall—almost as tall as the trees—and so skinny that they lived in the cracks of the rocks.

Michael Christie (1985) at a literal translation, preserving the Aboriginal idiom and mode of storytelling used by one of the old people from Milingimbi:

> More people came on horses. 'Hey! Let's go and have a look on the plains over there. We'll go and see if we can find some of the aboriginal people cooking on the plains over there.' And they went with ten horses.

The most obvious, recurring event in Aboriginal stories is the transformation of humans into animals, rocks, hills and other elements of the natural world. There is little difference, in fact, between humans and the natural world, because rivers and stones as well as birds and kangaroos possess a spirit. In the Dreamtime world, events occur in a dimension which takes no account of Western concepts of time, space and causality. What is significant is how the participants interact and the kind of psychological connections which underlie their relationships. Unlike Western concepts of story as a way of recalling past events, Aboriginal stories become a recreation of the original event.

The Quinkins by Percy Trezise and Dick Roughsey.

This is Still Rainbow Snake Country

This is a picture book of traditional oral stories from Western Arnhem Land which have been translated and written down by Catherine Berndt. The illustrations are by Raymond Meek who has adapted the typical forms and patterns of traditional Aboriginal art for book illustration using modern media.

The book also provides most useful background information about the people and places which are re-created in these stories. We are told something about Western Arnhem Land, about the history of the

77

Aboriginal people and the changes that have occurred. There is a guide to pronouncing key Aboriginal words which appear in the story, and a map which locates the stories in their physical environment.

Each story is amplified by a brief mention of the storyteller and the circumstances in which he or she first heard the story: 'This is one of the stories that Mangurug's father told her when she was a little girl.' These references serve to remind us that this particular retelling is simply one in a long chain. Berndt also frames the stories in much the same way as an oral storyteller with a live audience would do. She alerts the reader to the significance of what is to unfold, then follows up with relevant information which lends credibility to the story. These addendums often emerge as though in answer to the readers' question, for example: 'The place where this happened is called Mayaya-rung-bu, west of the East Alligator River'.

This is Still Rainbow Snake Country can be used in a variety of ways: to consider the difference between oral and written storytelling; as a basis for drama activities; and to give students an introduction to an Aboriginal perspective on the environment.

▶ Ask students to bring a family story to class to share with a small group. In telling the story they should offer information about where they first heard it and from whom and whether other versions of the story exist within the family.

▶ Encourage students to reflect on the value and personal significance of their stories. How are they used to maintain family solidarity and tradition? What are the values inherent in each story? How does the context of storytelling contribute to its meaning?

▶ After reading a number of Berndt's stories, divide the class into small groups. Give each student the opportunity to retell a favourite story. Encourage the storyteller to add or embellish while retaining the essence of the story. The audience should also be active participants, asking questions and making interjections. A group's version of the story can be written down.

▶ This activity may be followed by a discussion about the relationship between storyteller and audience — both in oral and written modes.

▶ Select particular stories for enactment. As well as enacting the events, students can explore the concept of transformation from human to animal or to inanimate forms. Experiment through movement or slow-motion sculptures with the notion that, although external appearance is transformed, the spirit is unchanged.

▶ Ask students to make a series of depictions of Galdadja, 'the rock sitting . . . on dry land', and Nawaran the snake-man who turned into a rock together with his spears, spear-thrower and palm-leaf baskets.

▶ Create a landscape using the map on page 15. People it with characters from the various stories, then introduce an alien element: the farmer, the miner, the tourist.

▶ Encourage the students to create an improvised scene. Then de-role the students.

The Peopling of Australia

This is a picture book with both text and pictures by Percy Trezise. It uses the genre of a history rather than a narrative, presenting a chronicle of Australia before white people arrived. The book is an attempt to explore Australia's past using concepts of time and space which can be understood by the average non-Aboriginal reader. In describing the evolution of Aboriginal societies, Trezise continually points to the interdependence between people and the environment. This is most evident in the pictures which use the landscape rather than people as the focus. All the human figures are scaled according to their relative size within the landscape. There are no visual tricks, no foreshortening, no enlargement of detail. We see into these paintings as if we were part of the world they depict. Trezise has used colours with the intention of recording the appearance of things faithfully, so that the overall effect is like a naive painting.

This book can be used to stimulate discussion about people and the environment, about how history is written, and about the relationship between history, myth, and the origin of religion.

▶ Read *The Peopling of Australia* to the students.
▶ Ask students to produce a time-line of the dates offered in the picture book. List the signposts which mark significant steps in the peopling of Australia.
▶ Make a summary of people's attitudes to animals. What conclusions can be drawn about Aboriginal husbandry from the law: 'No one must ever kill an animal made poor by drought. In drought everything must become poor, including man, so that all may survive the hard times'?

The Peopling of Australia by Percy Trezise.

There was also danger from the still active volcanos and earthquakes. Race memory still recalls that the mountains exploded and the ground opened up and swallowed people.

There were fearful times when the whole earth trembled, the air was full of smoke and ash, and the sky a redness never seen before.

- Read the opening chapters of the Book of Genesis. Compare the biblical land of Eden and the place that God reserved for humans with the Aboriginal perspective.
- Examine current attitudes to the land. Make a list of the attitudes held by white people to their environment. For instance, consider the point of view that might be held by an executive of BHP, a conservationist, a timber worker, a city dweller. Examine some relevant Australian poetry, such as Henry Kendall's 'The Last of his Tribe', Bruce Dawe's 'Homo Suburbiensis', or Judith Wright's 'At Coololah'. How are these attitudes different from those in *The Peopling of Australia*?

Pigs and Honey

Pigs and Honey written and illustrated by Jeanie Adams is quite different from these two books. Both text and illustrations are firmly based in the genre of realism, telling the story of an Aboriginal family living in an unspecified rural location, who go on a camping trip.

One of the significant features of this book is that it shows the ordinary everyday life of an Aboriginal family in the 1980s. One is reminded of the books of Ezra Jack, such as *The Pet Show*, which portray characters of different ethnic backgrounds in a contemporary American setting. This family has adapted to both white and black culture and technology: they drive to the bush hunting grounds in a truck, but spear the pig with a woomera. The book is not offered as an explanation of one culture to another; instead it shows a family who have found their own accommodations. Perhaps the greatest value of this book is its ordinariness—for Aboriginal children to see a reflection of modern Aboriginal life with which they can identify, and for white children to see something other than the stereotypical images of an Aboriginal culture set firmly in the past.

Pigs and Honey allows for a number of comparisons and contrasts of different family structures and cultural practices.

- Have students make a list of all the types of food found by the various characters in the story. Compare this to a list of food they and their family would take on a camping weekend. What conclusions can be drawn about the different attitudes to food, its source and its preparation?
- Have students write a recipe for roast pork cooked in a bush oven.
- How does the family allocate tasks and responsibilities? What is the position of children, old people, women?

There is an interesting focus on place which has a strong base in Aboriginal culture. Jeanie Adams gives precise details about the direction of the journey and describes the landscape in detail. There is even an illustration which is an aerial view of the 'dinner camp site'.

- Ask students to draw a map pointing to significant landforms.

Pigs and Honey is narrated by one of the children, but the language, though colloquial is mostly standard English. There are some unlucky phrases such as 'sure enough' and 'we trudged back'

Granny and the little kids stayed there at the dinner camp. Mum and Aunty started looking around straight away for wild honey. They shaded their eyes against the sun as they looked for the tiny bees flying to their hives in the tree-tops. Grandad made a bough shade for the kids, and Granny made a fire to boil tea.

After a while old Grandad called out, "We're getting close now. See the well over there?" So Uncle stopped the truck in a clear place on high ground, not far from the swamp, and we all jumped out.

which don't seem to fit the narrator's voice. Discussion of the author's task—how to preserve a credible narrative voice while producing a commercial product—would lead naturally into a variety of writing tasks.

Pigs and Honey by Jeanie Adams.

▶ Ask students to write conversations using non-standard forms of English, such as the language used by teenagers or grandparents. The reference to Granny and her stories around the campfire could lead to further writing or retelling experiences using colloquial, oral language.
▶ Ask students to write their own picture story book about a camping weekend, using some of the devices from *Pigs and Honey*.

Other books that could be explored on this topic include:
- *The Rainbow Serpent*   Percy Trezise & Dick Roughsey
- *Turramulli The Giant Quinkin*   Percy Trezise & Dick Roughsey
- *The Magic Firesticks*   Percy Trezise & Dick Roughsey
- *The Giant Devil Dingo*   Dick Roughsey (Percy Trezise and Dick Roughsey have produced a number of titles similar to those above.)
- *The Rainbow Serpent*   Oodgeroo Noonuccal & Kabul Oodgeroo Noonuccal
- *The Aboriginal Children's History of Australia*
- *the tintookies and little fella bindi*   Peter Scriven
- *Tiddalick*   Robert Roennfeldt
- *Djet*   Wakuthi Marawili
- *Father Sky and Mother Earth*   Kath Walker

NESB Perspective

A common difficulty that teachers find with students from non-English-speaking backgrounds (NESB) in upper primary and secondary classes is the gap that exists between students' oral communication in English and their literacy skills in English. These different proficiencies in English are quite commonly referred to as BICS (Basic Interpersonal Communicative Skills) and CALP (Cognitive Academic Language Proficiency), terms introduced by Jim Cummins (1984). Although there is a danger of using labels like this too readily, they do emphasise the gap that is never bridged for some children. Any teachers of second- or third-phase learners of English would be familiar with such differences and understand the ways many second-language learners are disadvantaged in their ability to achieve success in literary and academic tasks at school.

It is therefore even more important for NESB students that they be given a context for their reading. This context may involve building on students' background knowledge and 'filling in the gaps' in the text. This can be done by using picture books in three different ways:

- choosing picture books in which the pictures actually provide the context;
- choosing picture books in which the context needs to be filled in, thus providing students with further interpretation techniques that will enable them to become more independent readers for other reading;
- applying a 'communicative' approach.

To complete these activities you will need copies of the following picture books:

- *Where the Wild Things Are*   Maurice Sendak
- *Wilfrid Gordon McDonald Partridge*   Mem Fox & Julie Vivas
- *Waiting for May*   Thryza Davey
- *Kirsty Knows Best*   Annalena McAfee & Anthony Browne
- *Through the Magic Mirror*   Anthony Browne
- *Gorilla*   Anthony Browne
- *Mr Nick's Knitting*   Margaret Wild & Dee Huxley
- *The Angel with a Mouth Organ*   Christobel Mattingley & Astra Lacis
- *Piggybook*   Anthony Browne
- *The Moon's Revenge*   Joan Aiken & Alan Lee
- *Kojuro and the Bears*   Junko Morimoto
- *The Jolly Postman*   Janet & Allan Ahlberg

---

*P*ICTURE BOOKS THAT PROVIDE A CONTEXT FOR THE READER

Multicultural Texts

Unfortunately there is a distinct lack of picture books that reflect the experiences of different migrant or nationality groups in Australia. The few that portray life in other countries tend to depict stereotyped images, for example *Nini at the Carnival* or *Ayu and the Perfect Moon*. Nadia Wheatley and Donna Rawlins' *My Place* is an important exception that is certain to influence other writers in the future. There are also few Australian picture books with illustrations that include people from ethnic backgrounds other than Anglo-Saxon.

▶ In groups, ask students to discuss the possible ways in which different nationality groups could be represented in picture books, for example:
  • stories set in countries of origin, and based either in the past or in a contemporary setting;
  • stories that focus on the migrant experience of particular groups in Australia, either in recent history or now;
  • stories that include different nationality groups in a contemporary setting in Australia, particularly different generations.
▶ Ask students to research the history of different migrant groups in Australia, incorporating documents, photos or illustrations. Other students could attempt some writing and/or illustrating of their own picture books to incorporate some or all of the above.
▶ Collect and read folk tales from other countries. Do these help to provide a context for NESB readers?

Providing a Context

There are many picture books for older children that provide a context for the reader, particularly through the pictures. In these books the pictures fill in the gaps for readers and in some cases provide a concrete basis for readers to understand the imaginative or abstract references of the author. These picture books could be utilised with NESB students to create a reading experience that is enjoyable and understandable.

▶ Using *Where the Wild Things Are*, have students look at the illustrations for exact details, not given in the verbal text, of Max's naughtiness, and then of his journey. Discuss how the author is using illustrations to lead the reader to 'imagine'.
▶ In pairs or small groups, ask students to choose various imaginative recreations:
  • Describe or draw different details of Max making 'mischief of one kind or another'.
  • Describe or draw a different journey from that depicted in the illustrations to 'the place where the wild things are'.
  • Write the events of 'the night' from Max's mother's point of view.

till Max said "BE STILL!"
and tamed them with the magic trick

of staring into all their yellow eyes without blinking once
and they were frightened and called him the most wild thing of all

Where the Wild Things Are
by Maurice Sendak.

- Rewrite the story so that some description or reference is made to the changes in the moon that are shown in the illustrations.
- Conduct a TV interview between Max and a reporter, imagining that he has been found after being reported missing by his mother.
- Dramatically depict through movement how Max's room changes to become 'the world all around'.

▶ Have students discuss the abstract nature of the language: 'in and out of weeks', 'almost over a year'. What is Sendak trying to have the reader imagine? How would these words work without pictures? Look for other examples of abstract language like this in poetry, and try illustrating these images.

▶ Using *Wilfrid Gordon McDonald Partridge*, ask groups of students to dramatically enact each of the memories of Miss Nancy.

▶ Discuss how the technique of flashback is used through the combination of words and pictures. How different is this from the way flashback is used in filming? Try putting some of the flashback in this book into words.

▶ Have students consider the way flashback can be used by novelists (an easy example is used at the beginning of Betsy Byars' *The Midnight Fox*).

▶ Write part of a film script where flashback is used.

▶ Discuss how readers understand the emotional bond between Wilfrid Gordon and Miss Nancy.

▶ For a thematic link, a similar bond between a young boy and an old man is developed in the picture book in chapter form, *Waiting for May* by Thyrza Davey. Students could compare how this theme is developed through a more extensive use of narrative. Discuss how the illustrations work to highlight events rather than fill in details for the reader.

▶ Find examples of difficult language in the text. How could you illustrate these to explain the theme? Other aspects of this theme could be explored through debates, researching articles in the media, finding other poems and stories on the topic.

PICTURE BOOKS THAT NEED THE CONTEXT FILLED IN

As we have discussed in Part 1, there are many picture books that contain subtleties for the reader. Such picture books may be just as difficult as novels for second language learners because the reader has to fill in the gaps. Yet the pictures do provide more 'filling in' than the decontextualised aspects of some novels. A shared reading of these books with teachers or peers can help students in such cases.

▶ Before reading some of these picture books have the students imagine themselves in another time or place, even in a legend they may have heard of. Ask them to write a description of the time and place, and illustrate it if possible. Compare this with their real everyday lives.

To what extent does a book like *Kirsty Knows Best* become decontextualised because of the nature of the relationship between picture and text?

Would NESB students understand the fantasies of Kirsty that fluctuate between taking her back to the days of medieval princesses then to the legend of the Willow Pattern Plate, and then back to the present time for Kirsty? How is the context provided for the reader here—before or after reading? Can such activities help with other reading skills and lead a reader into other stages of reader-response?

Picture books can also be a way of introducing a topic or theme before studying a novel. For example, reading *Granpa* or *John Brown, Rose and the Midnight Cat* can be a good introduction to novels that deal with death, such as *Bridge to Terabithia* or *Papa's Going to Buy You a Mocking Bird*. In this case the picture book provides an interesting context for the theme of the novel. Picture books can also be useful to assist NESB students with the study of Shakespeare (see pages 90 to 96).

APPLYING A COMMUNICATIVE APPROACH

Recent research into second language learning has shown that second language learners benefit more from learning through a 'communicative' approach. Such an approach creates real situations where language will occur naturally, and where language is generated as a result of the activity. The focus is not on the activity itself, but rather on the language and the thinking that develops as a result of the activity.

Some communicative activities could be applied to picture books as a way of generating language related to the literature and also to encourage thinking around the texts. They are particularly designed as pair or group tasks where interaction will occur with discussion of features of the text.

Communicative activities are sometimes divided into 'collaborative' or 'information gap' activities (NSW Department of Education 1984). Collaborative activities are those in which the students all have the same information and work together to make decisions or form conclusions. Information gap activities are those in which students have different information from each other, and have to exchange information to complete the task. Barrier games are common information gap activities.

While both these types of activities can be used with picture books and are suggested here, they should not be applied too rigidly. Below are some suggestions that may generate reading response in a different way by applying aspects of second-language teaching curricula. There are many ways of approaching picture books. All of the other suggested approaches in this book are just as applicable and valid for second language learners, especially when the teacher is aware of the gaps in language that may be preventing students from reaching academic proficiency in response to literature.

Collaborative Activities

Identify
▶ Using *Through the Magic Mirror*, identify the different surreal images on each page. Discuss how this evokes humour.

Observe and Comment
▶ Using *Gorilla*, identify where the illustrations change from the real to the fantastic to represent the dreaming of Hannah. Is there anywhere that these merge so that there is ambiguity about whether it is dream or reality?
▶ Using *Kirsty Knows Best*, consider how Anthony Browne uses the motif of Nora's hairstyle to recur in other shapes, particularly heads, through many of the illustrations. What do you think Browne is trying to say to his reader through this illustration?

Present and Justify
▶ Using *Mr Nick's Knitting*, suggest the author's purpose behind the story. Justify your answer by commenting on how this is shown through the text and illustrations.

Hypothesise and Reason
▶ Discuss the parallel between the war-time experience and Christmas made in *The Angel with a Mouth Organ*.

Classify
▶ Using a variety of picture books, identify how illustrators convey realism or fantasy, mood, atmosphere, point of view or humour.

Information Gap Activities

Problem-solving
▶ Using *Mr Nick's Knitting*, read the story to the point at which Mr Nick visits Mrs Jolley in hospital. Ask students to discuss what they would do for Mrs Jolley if they were Mr Nick. Have them write (or illustrate) alternatives and then compare these with the illustrations in the book.

Information-sharing
▶ In a small group, read Anthony Browne's *Piggybook* then complete the reproducible co-operative cloze activity on page 89. The words that emphasise the comparison of the humans with animals have been deleted. Discuss, then explain how these words contribute to the satire in the book.
▶ Consider how much the illustrations support and extend the satirical metamorphosis.

Rank Ordering
▶ Construct a plot profile of *The Moon's Revenge*. Discuss how predictable this plot development is. Try making a plot profile for an unwritten story which you may or may not choose to write.

Enquiry and Elimination
▶ Using *Kojuro and the Bears*, decide which picture represents the most climactic part of the story. Compare the content in each picture and the variation of colour and line to justify your decision.

Matrix
▶ Using *The Jolly Postman*, have students complete the reproducible matrix on page 88, detailing the events in the postman's journey, as well as the characteristics of the language used in each episode. Students need to summarise events here, but also to consider the varieties of media used for letter writing. Note how the level of language changes to suit each form. Once familiar with this type of activity, you could devise matrix activities based on different books.

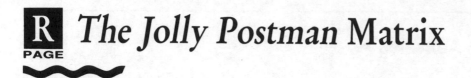

The Jolly Postman Matrix

▶ Read *The Jolly Postman.*
▶ The Jolly Postman makes six stops on his journey. For each stop, fill in the details on the matrix below.

Stops on the Jolly Postman's journey	First	Second	Third	Fourth	Fifth	Sixth
Fairy story the character comes from						
Number of people present						
Type of drink						
The postman's feelings						
Genre of letter						
Register of language						

The next day and the next night and the day after that, Mrs Piggott was still not there.

Mr Piggott, Simon and Patrick _____ to look after themselves.

They never _____ the dishes. They never

_____ their clothes. Soon the house was like a _____.

'When is Mum coming home?' the boys _____ after another horrible meal.

'How should I know?' Mr Piggott _____.

They all became more and more _____. One night there was nothing in the

house for them to cook.

'We'll just have to _____ around and find some _____,

_____ Mr Piggott. And just then Mrs Piggott walked in.

Shakespeare and Picture Books

The Wedding Ghost by
Leon Garfield and Charles
Keeping.

This section differs somewhat from the previous sections in Part 2, in that the picture books discussed are linked in one way or another with the study of some of Shakespeare's plays. The emphasis of the activities is on allowing students to connect aspects of familiar picture books with aspects of the study of some of the plays, rather than on reading picture books for their own sake.

To complete these activities, you will need copies of some or all of the following picture books:

- *Hansel and Gretel*   Anthony Browne
- *The Boy Who Cried Wolf*   Tony Ross
- *Angelo*   Quentin Blake
- *Bear Hunt*   Anthony Browne
- *A Lion in the Meadow*   Margaret Mahy
- *Lulu and the Flying Babies*   Posy Simmonds
- *The Story of Chicken Licken*   Jan Ormerod
- *Rosie's Walk*   Pat Hutchins
- *Piggybook*   Anthony Browne
- *The Paper Bag Princess*   Robert Munsch &
    Michael Martchenko
- *Princess Smartypants*   Babette Cole
- *Outside Over There*   Maurice Sendak
- *The Wedding Ghost*   Leon Garfield & Charles Keeping

This is by no means an exhaustive list. Connections could be made between the witches in books such as Mem Fox's *Guess What?* and the witches in *Macbeth*.

A tedious brief scene of young Pyramus
And his love Thisbe; very tragical mirth.
Merry and tragical? Tedious and brief?
That is hot ice and wondrous strange snow.
How shall we find the concord of this discord?
Theseus, *A Midsummer Night's Dream*,
act 5, scene 1

Shakespeare and picture books in the secondary English classroom would seem to be a discord of major proportions, yet the differences may all too easily mask the areas of concordance.

Borrowed Plots

Shakespeare, as we all know, borrowed the stories for his plays from a variety of sources. His audience knew the stories. What they came to the theatre to see was what the dramatist did with the tale. Originality, while highly valued today, has not been so highly prized in other times. Moreover there is an excitement in seeing a known story transposed into a new setting, or given a new ending. There are now a wealth of picture books available that amply demonstrate how a well-known tale can be given new layers of meaning in a retelling.

Anthony Browne's retelling of *Hansel and Gretel* is a particularly fine example of this. Browne retells the folk tale with illustrations that place it firmly in the twentieth century. The avarice of the stepmother is illustrated through the objects with which she is associated: cosmetics, perfumes and stockings. Through the pictures she is linked with the wicked witch in the forest.

Tony Ross's *The Boy Who Cried Wolf* is another book which illustrates the retelling of a well-known story. Ross, through clever satiric pictures and the altered ending, points the irony of this tale. This is no more or less than Shakespeare did with most of his stories. Duncan, for instance, was not a good king in reality, but something of a tyrant. Shakespeare's portrayal of him as a good and virtuous man works to contrast the horror of his murder.

▶ Ask students to recall the story of *Hansel and Gretel*.
▶ Introduce the original version from one of the Grimm's Fairy Tale editions.
▶ Introduce the Anthony Browne version.
▶ Discuss the differences that appear in the two versions.
▶ Ask students to imagine how Shakespeare might have presented the story of *Hansel and Gretel* in a play.
▶ Ask students to find another well-known tale and to retell it in a modern setting.

Commedia dell' Arte

Not only did Shakespeare borrow his stories from various sources, he was quite eclectic in the way he used dramatic techniques. His was not naturalistic theatre. The size and shape of the stage allowed for a variety of actions. *Commedia dell' arte* was one source from which he borrowed. The stock characters, the courtly love, the pranks and tricks and general physicality of *commedia* appear in many of his plays, particularly in the clown characters, once thought to have been included only to keep the groundlings entertained.

Angelo, by Quentin Blake, illustrates something of the flavour of this style of theatre, not only in the illustrations of the performers, but also in the love story itself. It is the tale of a beautiful young girl locked away in a tower, and rescued eventually by the young Angelo, a performer in a travelling troupe. This little tale echoes the story of Jessica and Lorenzo from *The Merchant of Venice*.

> What, are there masques? Hear you me Jessica:
> Lock up my doors, and when you hear the drum,
> And the vile squealing of the wry-neck'd fife,
> Clamber not you up to the casements then,
> Nor thrust your head into the public street
> To gaze on Christian fools with varnish'd faces.
>
> Shylock, *The Merchant of Venice*,
> act 2, scene 5

▶ Share the story of *Angelo* with the class.
▶ Discuss the types of *commedia* activities that the troupe engages in.
▶ Devise a *commedia*-style scene that plays out the story of the princess rescued from the tower.
▶ Read the scenes from *Merchant of Venice* that involve Jessica and Lorenzo, particularly her escape from her father's house.
▶ Discuss the ways in which this scene might be enlivened by the *commedia* activities.

Stories as Created Constructs

In Elizabethan times the dramatist openly acknowledged to his audience that he was making a play. The prologue to many of his plays remind the audience of this. This is a notion that runs counter to many students' perceptions of theatre. Although it is once again becoming a feature of contemporary drama, naturalistic theatre and the realism of much television does not work from this basis. Realistic drama works from the assumption that the audience accepts that it is real. The audience are voyeurs looking into a scene that is enacted before their eyes. However there is no communication between players and audience.

This was not the case in Elizabethan theatre. The notion of the work of art being created and the creation being acknowledged to the audience is well illustrated in the delightful book by Anthony Browne, *Bear Hunt*. Here we see Bear using a pencil to draw his way out of many difficult situations as two hunters chase him in the forest. As Bear draws, the reader is reminded that this is a story being made. This is further highlighted through the landscape that Browne uses to highlight the irony of his story—a landscape filled with lightbulbs, life-saving rings, matches, an American flag, cups, jugs and so on.

Stories as created constructs is also the subject of Margaret Mahy's *A Lion in the Meadow*. Here Mahy demonstrates the power of the imagination in creating characters of monstrous porportions.

- Ask the students to define what they mean by reality. Explore their definitions.
- Ask students how real they think the action of a play on stage is.
- Ask students to define art.
- Read *A Lion in the Meadow* by Margaret Mahy, and *Lulu and the Flying Babies* by Posy Simmonds.
- Discuss the notions of the work of art, or literature as they appear in these stories.
- Examine some of the prologues or epilogues to Shakespeare's plays, and the play within the play in a play in *A Midsummer Night's Dream*. What similar ideas are highlighted here?

Dual Action

The size and shape of the Elizabethan stage allowed for quite complex dramatic action. Characters were able to eavesdrop on the activities of other characters. Great ball scenes, battle scenes, and processions could be accommodated. Intimate scenes of love were also possible. Perhaps one of the most commonly used devices is the scene of dual action. This often appears in the form of the play within the play, as in *Hamlet* and *A Midsummer Night's Dream*, where two sets of actions are happening simultaneously, and the audience is aware of both simultaneously.

A similar device is used in Jan Ormerod's retelling of *The Story of Chicken Licken*, in which a play is being enacted on the stage of a school hall. It is of course the play of Chicken Licken being enacted by children. The illustrations are drawn from the perspective of the rear of the audience. The reader is aware not only of the action that is happening on the stage, but also the action that is happening in the front row of the audience where a baby crawls out of its bassinet and eventually joins the action on the stage.

- Read *The Story of Chicken Licken* to the class and examine how the two narratives co-exist.
- Compare this with Shakespeare's use of play within the play.

Dramatic Irony

Dramatic irony is another common device employed by Shakespeare. It is quite usual for the audience to be privy to information that characters on the stage do not know. For instance, Bottom unknowingly appears with an ass's head which Puck has placed there as a trick; Bassanio and Gratiano are unaware that the doctor and clerk to whom they give the rings are their own wives in disguise; Malvolio is oblivious to the fact that the letter of love is not from Olivia, but a forgery by Maria.

One of the most entertaining little picture books that employs this device is *Rosie's Walk* by Pat Hutchins. In this tale the verbal text tells of Rosie's walk around the farmyard. The visual text shows the fox who is stalking her, and the strife he encounters in the process. The reader does not know whether Rosie is aware of the presence of the fox.

▶ Read the words of *Rosie's Walk* to the class without showing the pictures.
▶ Discuss the story that appears to be happening.
▶ Reread the story showing the pictures.
▶ Discuss the difference this has made to the audience.

Gender Roles

Picture books may also provide fodder for the issues raised in particular plays. One of Shakespeare's most entertaining comedies is *The Taming of the Shrew*. This play raises a number of issues about gender roles and expectations. These issues are also the subject of another book by Anthony Browne called *Piggybook*. In this delightfully constructed tale, it is the males who are in need of civilising. Browne presents the reader with a complex text where the motif of the pig appears in a variety of contexts, building to the crescendo which depicts the males as the pigs of the piece. Their taming is essential to the ultimate harmony of the household, however it is a different sort of taming to Kate's.

▶ Read *Piggybook*, *The Paper Bag Princess* and *Princess Smartypants* to the class.
▶ Discuss the issues that these raise.
▶ Compare the views of women here with the views of women expressed in *The Taming of the Shrew*.

> I am asham'd that women are so simple
> To offer war where they should kneel for peace;
> Or seek for rule, supremacy and sway,
> When they are bound to serve, love and obey.
> > Katherine, *The Taming of the Shrew*,
> > act 5, scene 2

Fairies and Goblins

Fairies and goblins appear in many of Shakespeare's plays, notably *The Tempest* and *A Midsummer Night's Dream*. Students' perceptions of these creatures has often been moulded by the romantic images of twee little tinselly creatures with glistening wings. These are not the fairies that people Shakespeare's plays.

> I am that merry wanderer of the night.
> I jest to Oberon, and make him smile
> When I a fat and bean-fed horse beguile,
> Neighing in likeness of a filly foal;

And sometimes lurk I in a gossip's bowl,
In very likeness of a roasted crab,
And when she drinks, against her lips I bob,
And on her wither'd dewlap pour the ale.

Puck, A Midsummer Night's Dream,
act 2, scene 1

Tricksters such as Puck and Ariel are the sorts of characters that Maurice Sendak has drawn in his picture book *Outside Over There*. This is the story of a changeling child. Goblins steal Ida's sister and replace her with the changeling. Ida sets out on a quest for the child whom she eventually retrieves from their clutches by playing her magic horn. Sendak's illustrations effectively show the nature of the goblins. They are faceless creatures. They appear everywhere. The reader is aware of them, but the characters are not. The music of Ida's horn is a motif comparable with the music used by Ariel to lure Ferdinand to Prospero. But this time it is the human child who is luring the goblins.

Outside Over There by Maurice Sendak.

This music crept by me upon the waters,
Allaying both their fury and my passion
With its sweet air; thence have I followed it,
Or it hath drawn me rather.

Ferdinand, The Tempest,
act 1, scene 2

The changeling child is the basis of the fight between Oberon and Titania in *A Midsummer Night's Dream*. As Puck tells us,

She never had so sweet a changeling—
And jealous Oberon would have the child
Knight of his train, to trace the forests wild.

Puck, A Midsummer Night's Dream,
act 2, scene 1

Sendak's book allows students to explore these issues and to relate them to the plays.

▶ Read *Outside Over There* and compare the visions of the fairies in it with the fairies from Shakespeare's plays.

The Wedding Ghost and Twelfth Night

The connection between the issues and story of one of the plays has been made quite deliberately by Charles Keeping and Leon Garfield in their haunting tale, *The Wedding Ghost*. Garfield and Keeping preface this book with Feste's song from the second act of *Twelfth Night*—'O mistress mine! Where are you roaming?' This song, which encapsulates some of the key issues of the play, poses questions about the nature of love, time, youth and the satisfying of present needs. This story interweaves the lines of the poem in a repeated pattern within the framework of the story of the Sleeping Beauty, culminating in the repetition of 'Then come and kiss me, sweet and twenty', as Jack awakens the Sleeping Beauty with a kiss. This complex story connects at a number of points with the play. For instance, as Jack ponders over delaying the kiss we are reminded of Feste's song to Orsino.

> It was death either way; it was death to go, death to stay.
> Come away, come away, death;
> And in sad cypress let me be laid;
> Fly away, fly away, breath,
> I am slain by a fair cruel maid.
>
> Feste, *Twelfth Night*,
> act 2, scene 4

There are a number of key issues in *Twelfth Night* which are also explored in *The Wedding Ghost*. Disguise, deception and self-deception are important ideas in both. Jack, in kissing the Princess, faces his hidden desire, but is left haunted as a result. Echoing the words of Lady Macbeth after the murder of Duncan, the narrator tells us, 'What he had done, could not be undone.' Jack's plight at the end reminds us also of other songs of Feste, in particular,

> I'll be with you again,
> In a trice,
> Like to the old Vice,
> Your need to sustain.
> *The Wedding Ghost*

and the final song of the play,

> But when I came, alas! to wive,
> With hey, ho, the wind and the rain,
> By swaggering could I never thrive,
> For the rain it raineth every day.
>
> Feste, *Twelfth Night*,
> act 5, scene 1

It is well worth spending time reading *The Wedding Ghost* before exploring these plays of Shakespeare.

Picture books and Shakespeare's plays ('no epilogue, I pray you; for your play needs no excuse') make a happy marriage in the secondary classroom. The juxtaposition of these two elevates both in value. Picture books demystify the apparent distance and complexity of the Shakespearean text by assisting in the process of visualisation. At the same time the plays highlight the complexity of the ideas and devices of the picture book genre.

Theme Study:
People and Nature

Picture books deal with this theme in a variety of ways and teachers can approach this topic from different perspectives depending on the level of the class and their own objectives. The following are some suggestions.

> To complete these activities you will need copies of the following picture books:
> - *The Bunyip of Berkeley's Creek*   Jenny Wagner & Ron Brooks
> - *The Ox-Cart Man*   Donald Hall & Barbara Cooney
> - *Goanna*   Jenny Wagner & Noela Hills
> - *Where the Forest Meets the Sea*   Jeannie Baker

The Bunyip of Berkeley's Creek

This is a delightful story about a creature of Aboriginal fantasy, the Bunyip, who finally finds another Bunyip 'just like me'. We see a fascinating interplay of fantasy and reality as the Bunyip searches for what could be seen as recognition, self-identity and friendship. Within this narrative framework, the book adds density by the way it requires a reader to 'fill in gaps'. It's whole meaning is multi-layered, especially as it is expressed through the pictures.

In pairs or groups ask students to discuss the following aspects of the book.
- Look closely at the illustration of the one human being in this story. Consider the way this man is represented, both in his exterior and interior environment.
- How does the environment of this man compare with the way the landscape of the Bunyip and the other animals is illustrated?
- Study the way colour and line are used to represent differences in both environments, and in the nature of the illustrations. What inferences is the reader meant to make about this man, and people in general?

- ▶ Trace the use of darkness and light in the illustrations of the Bunyip's journey along the creek.
- ▶ Discuss the irony in both the words and pictures when the man tells the Bunyip that 'Bunyips simply don't exist' while he is described as 'looking straight through' the Bunyip.
- ▶ What might the writer be saying in this book about fantasy and reality?
- ▶ Compare the man's attitude towards the Bunyip with the attitude of the other animals.
- ▶ Consider the use of language in this book: both the voice of the narrator and the use of dialogue.
- ▶ To what extent is the reader led to 'fill in gaps' — to contrast nature with science; dream with reality, as the Bunyip wanders back into the 'natural' landscape to his waterhole? It is back at the billabong, when the Bunyip seems to have given up hope of friendship or reassurance — and when the reader may be ready to believe that Bunyips don't exist — that another Bunyip crawls out of the billabong. How does the reader respond to this?
- ▶ Compare this book with the way nature is ravaged by human technology in *The Bear Who Wanted to Stay a Bear*.
- ▶ Ask students to write imaginative re-creations of either story, i.e. to rewrite either story story from the point of view of the Bunyip or the Bear.

The Ox-Cart Man

This book offers an interesting contrast to *The Bear Who Wanted to Stay a Bear* in that both books represent changes in people's relationship with nature in different centuries. The cycle of the seasons in which people live in harmony with nature is suggested by this simple story of rural life blended with illustrations of nineteenth century rural New England.
- ▶ How well do the illustrations capture the atmosphere of this place and period? Research this topic to find other art representations of this time and place.
- ▶ Does the choice of colours/line suit the particular story? In what way?
- ▶ Ask students to use artwork from a particular period or their own illustrations to make their own picture book.
- ▶ Find illustrations of a specific place from a particular period. Use these to write the story of a picture book.

Goanna and *Where the Forest Meets the Sea*

Both these books are very obviously concerned with the topic of conservation in Australia. *Goanna* is a book selected by the Australian Conservation Foundation, and *Where the Forest Meets the Sea* has focused attention on the importance of the preservation of the rainforest in the Daintree area of North Queensland. At the same time both books are quite different in their artistic presentation of this theme.

▶ Ask students to find out more information on the Daintree rainforest. What plans have been made by developers and how has the Government reacted to any such proposals?

▶ Investigate other natural areas in Australia that may be under similar threat.

▶ Graphs could be made of changes that have occurred in the ecology of selected areas over time.

▶ Encourage group presentations of these areas of research, and also debates. Guest speakers, representing either point of view, might be invited if possible.

▶ Letters or petitions could be written on an individual or class level.

▶ Compare the way the artwork of each book suits the book's subject matter. Each book uses collage, although Jeannie Baker's is much more extensive. Consider the effect of her collage being composed entirely of materials from the Daintree area. (A video has been made of the making of the book.) How does her use of collage suit this book, compared with the collage of non-natural materials that are superimposed on the landscape in some of the pages in *Goanna*?

▶ Consider how the artwork in *Where the Forests Meets the Sea* creates the perspective of past, present and future.

▶ Compare *Where the Forests Meets the Sea* with other books by Jeannie Baker that are illustrated with collage (e.g. *Millicent* and *Home in the Sky*). How does the artwork in these books suit their subject matter?

▶ In both books, discuss whether the theme is conveyed more in the words of the text or in the pictures.

▶ How strong is the characterisation of Goanna in the story? Does his character develop in itself or mainly serve the author's message? Do his reptilian characteristics suit the theme?

▶ Compare the contrasting colours in the Goanna's landscape early in the story with the change of colours that occurs as developers take over the environment. What is the effect of the unusual angles used in the few illustrations of the road and town toward the end?

Theme Study:
Families

The picture books in this section are used as a resource to stimulate the students to think about the issues associated with families, and to provide models of writing activities.

Wilfrid Gordon McDonald Partridge by Mem Fox.

To complete these activities you will need copies of some or all of the following books:

- *The Very Worst Monster*   Pat Hutchins
- *I'll Take You to Mrs Cole*   Nigel Gray & Michael Foreman
- *Don't Get Burnt*   Jack Bedson & Peter Gouldthorpe
- *Hansel and Gretel*   Anthony Browne
- *The Visitors Who Came to Stay*   Annalena McAfee & Anthony Browne
- *Why Do Grown-Ups Have All the Fun?*   Marisabina Russo
- *Wilfrid Gordon McDonald Partridge*   Men Fox & Julie Vivas
- *Granpa*   John Burningham
- *Sunshine*   Jan Ormerod
- *Moonlight*   Jan Ormerod
- *Crusher is Coming*   Bob Graham
- *Horrible Humans—A Field Guide*   Max Dann & Peter Viska

Family Roles and Stereotypes

▶ Ask students to bring in to class a family portrait photograph of their family. Allow time for students to share their photographs in small groups with other students. Encourage them to describe the individual members of the family and to talk about the relationships between individual members of the family.

▶ Ask students to write a description of any family members who are not in the photograph—for instance, grandparents or cousins. Allow time for students to share their descriptions with each other.

▶ Ask students to draw a family tree of their family for as far back as they can remember. Allow time for students to share these, noting similarities and differences.

▶ Ask each student to write a description of the family they will have in the future.

▶ Divide the class into small groups and ask each group to draw up a profile of the ideal mother, father, brother, sister, aunt, uncle, grandmother, grandfather, cousin. Negotiate category headings such as description, likes, dislikes, pastimes, favourite activities, etc. Suggest that each group finds a picture from a magazine to illustrate their description. Allow time for each group to share their pieces with the rest of the class.

▶ Now read the section of *Horrible Humans* entitled 'Humans of the Home'. Compare the students' descriptions with those of this text. In what ways are they similar? In what ways do they differ?

▶ Ask the students to rewrite their descriptions in a satiric form and to find an appropriate illustration to match the satiric version. Allow time for the students to share the results of their writing with the rest of the class.

▶ Collect the pieces and 'publish' these either in book form or as a series of posters.

Brothers and Sisters

▶ Divide the class into groups of three or four. Ask students who have younger brothers or sisters to tell anecdotes about their siblings. Each group will then select one of the stories told in the small group to share with the rest of the class. Ask the students to listen to the stories being told. What similarities and differences are evident? Are younger siblings seen as more of a nuisance than a joy?

▶ Read *Crusher is Coming* without showing the students the pictures. Ask them to imagine what is happening in the pictures in this book.

▶ Divide the class into pairs. Give each pair the verbal text for one of the double-page spreads in this book and ask them to draw the picture that they imagine could go with the words. Allow time for the students to share their pictures and to discuss the reasons for the choices that they have made. Encourage discussion of the way that Peter views his sister Claire, and his relationship with Crusher, and with his mother.

▶ Read the book again showing the illustrations and allowing time for the students to discuss some of the actions in the illustrations such as the mother kissing Peter, and Crusher playing with Claire.

▶ Look very closely at the back cover. In what way has Peter's relationship with Claire changed as a result of Crusher's coming?

Happy Families

Moonlight and *Sunshine*

▶ Select some of the key images from these two books, e.g. father burning the toast, reading to the girl, rushing about getting ready for work, preparing for bed, and so on. Allocate a single picture to each student and ask them to write a description of this family. The descriptions could include the activities that they normally engage in, the nature of their interrelationships and so on. Alternatively, they could use the picture as the springboard for a story about this family. Allow time for the students to 'publish' their writing and to discuss it with each other.

▶ Read the two books to the students, allowing time to discuss the sort of family this is, and to compare it with their own family situation. Is this family too idealised? Is the reality for the students quite different? Would they like to live in a family such as this one?

Why Do Grown-Ups Have all the Fun?

▶ Ask students to recall what happens at their bedtime. What do their parents do when they are in bed? How do parents react if they do not go to bed?

▶ Read this book to the class. Is this similar to their family situation? Is it too idealised?

Don't Get Burnt

▶ Ask students to recall situations where they have been on family picnics or a day at the beach with their family. Are these occasions always 'hassle-free'?

▶ Now read *Don't Get Burnt*. Allow time to discuss the family activities that are portrayed in this book.

Older Generations

Granpa
Wilfrid Gordon McDonald Partridge

▶ Divide the class into small groups. Ask the students in each group to describe their grandparents and the things that they do with their grandparents. If their grandparents are already deceased, ask them to recall their most precious memories of their grandparents. Allow time for the students to share with the class some of the stories from the small groups.

▶ Suggest that students contact their grandparents and ask them to recall some memories of their early childhood. The students could conduct an interview and tape their grandparents' voices. Ask students to retell these memories, or replay the tapes they have made. Allow time for discussion and comparison of these stories.

Perhaps students could make transcripts of the stories, and compare these with their own retellings.

▶ Divide students into groups and give each group one of the line drawings from *Granpa* that represents Granpa's memories. Ask each group of students to examine the picture closely. They should imagine that they are grandparents and write their account of this 'memory'. Allow time for each group to share their memories with the rest of the class.

▶ Divide the class into groups and give each group one of the metaphors for memories from *Wilfrid Gordon McDonald Partridge* — 'something warm', 'something from long ago', 'something that makes you cry', 'something that makes you laugh', 'something as precious as gold'. Ask each group to write a 'memory' that is congruent with their metaphor. Allow time for the groups to share their 'memories' with the rest of the class.

▶ Ask students to interview their grandparents for their warmest, funniest, most precious, etc., memories. Alternatively, take the class to an old people's home and allow the students to interview people there about their most precious memories.

▶ Now read the two books, *Granpa* and *Wilfrid Gordon McDonald Partridge*. Allow time for discussion of the images of grandparents and elderly people.

Blended Families

Hansel and Gretel
The Visitors Who Came to Stay

Students should have completed the family tree activity before going on with this section.

▶ Ask students to share their family trees and note any blended families. Allow time for students who are in blended family situations to discuss the experience — the positive and the negative aspects of this. Discuss the situations that might lead to such families being formed, e.g. death and divorce.

▶ Ask students in groups to draw up a profile of the stereotype of the wicked stepmother. This should include drawings or pictures. Allow time to share these with the rest of the class.

▶ Tell students the traditional tale of *Hansel and Gretel*. Discuss the image of the stepmother that the Grimm Brothers portray.

▶ Ask students to imagine that the story is set in modern times. Ask them to draw the stepmother as a modern character.

▶ Read Anthony Browne's *Hansel and Gretel*, allowing plenty of time to discuss the images that his retelling portrays.

▶ Read *The Visitors Who Came to Stay*, allowing time to discuss not only the issues associated with the blended family, but the ways in which Browne presents the 'joke' through the surrealistic illustrations.

Sibling Rivalry

The Very Worst Monster

▶ Ask students to recall times when they have felt jealous or envious of their siblings. Students should write an account of one incident when they have felt this way.

▶ Ask students to rewrite the incident from the point of view of the sibling. Allow time to share some of these occasions with the whole class.

▶ Read *The Very Worst Monster*. Discuss the presentation of sibling rivalry in this book. How does the cartoon format and the exaggeration soften the issue?

Eccentric Families

I'll Take You to Mrs Cole

▶ Not all families even attempt to conform to the stereotypical notions of families. Ask students if they know of any family situations that appear to be very unusual.

▶ Read *I'll Take You to Mrs Cole*. What sort of family is this? Are they happy?

Wilfrid Gordon McDonald Partridge by Mem Fox.

Author Study:
Anthony Browne

In this section students are encouraged to examine the work of a single writer as a whole. They are encouraged to construct in their own minds an image of the person they imagine would write these books. This may be complicated by the fact that an author may collaborate with an illustrator, or may illustrate the story of another author. Anthony Browne, for instance has collaborated with Annalena McAfee in the delightful story of *The Visitors Who Came to Stay*.

While this unit is designed around the work of Anthony Browne, it can be very readily adapted to explorations of other picture book writers such as Charles Keeping, Raymond Briggs, Junko Morimoto or Raymond Meeks. In adapting it to other authors it is desirable to select writers who develop both the visual and the verbal text for their picture books.

In this section students will be encouraged to work in groups, and in a variety of roles.

To complete these activities you will need copies of the following picture books by Anthony Browne:

- *Piggybook*
- *Hansel and Gretel*
- *Willy the Wimp*
- *Willy the Champ*
- *Gorilla*
- *The Visitors Who Came to Stay*
- *Kirsty Knows Best*
- *Through the Magic Mirror*

▶ Photocopy the reproducible activity sheets (pages 107 to 108) and distribute copies to groups of students.
▶ When all groups have completed their reports, publish them so that all members of the class have access to all reports.
▶ Convene a meeting of the entire panel or council to discuss the features of the reports. Encourage discussion of the features of the reports. Encourage discussion of the features noted in the reports. Ensure that the students stay in role as members of the panel or council so that they maintain an evaluative approach to the issues.
▶ What features are common to all reports? What differences are noted? Are these differences related to the books which Browne has

published on his own as opposed to those on which he has collaborated with Annalena McAfee?

▶ Ask students to take on the role of writers for a *Who's Who of Picture Book Writers*. They are to write the entry for Anthony Browne. Allow time for students to share their writing and to discuss their views of Anthony Browne the writer.

▶ Encourage students to write letters to Anthony Browne himself asking him for details about his writing, his ideas, his mode of writing. Compare the replies to these letters with the portraits they have constructed. Allow time for students to discuss their view of the writer in the books with the writer in the letters, and to evaluate his views and values with their own views of the world.

▶ Encourage students to research the work of Anthony Browne using books about illustrators and by writing letters to his publishers. Try to find out about his ideas and his modes of writing and illustrating. Compare the results with the portraits the students have constructed. Allow time for students to discuss their view of the writer with the information they have gained from their research, and to evaluate his views and values with their own views of the world.

Through the Magic Mirror by Anthony Browne.

Where was that mirror?

Author Study

Anthony Browne

In this study you will be working in small groups. You will also be working in role.

▶ In your group, choose *one* of the following activities:

1 Imagine that you are members of the Children's Book Council. As members of that Council, part of your job is to judge books that have been published for children. You will meet with other members of the Council, read the books allocated to you, and discuss them prior to writing a full report on them.

2 Imagine that you are members of an editorial panel for a publishing firm. You will meet with other members of the panel to discuss and evaluate the possibility of reprinting the books

allocated to you. You will also need to complete a written report.

▶ One of the following books will be allocated to each group:
Piggybook
Hansel and Gretel
Willy the Wimp
Willy the Champ
Gorilla
The Visitors Who Came to Stay
Kirsty Knows Best
Through the Magic Mirror

▶ After you have read the book together in your meeting, you should fill out the following report.

Book Report

Name of book _____

Author _____

Illustrator _____

Publisher _____

Date of publication and reprints _____

Type of picture book (e.g. illustrated, wordless, etc.) _____

Synopsis of narrative _____

_____

_____

The narrator _____

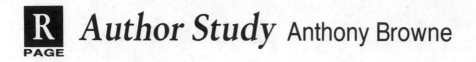

Author Study Anthony Browne

Nature of illustrations _____
_____
_____
_____

Main ideas raised by this book _____
_____

The characters in the narrative _____
_____
_____

How the characters are portrayed _____
_____
_____

The values that the book upholds _____
_____
_____

The tone of the book _____
_____

Recommendations for readership _____
_____
_____

Illustrator Study:
Maurice Sendak

The focus of this section is on the way a single illustrator can affect the tone of a book by changes in the style of illustration. While we have chosen the work of Maurice Sendak, it is possible to adapt these activities to any other illustrator.

To complete these activities you will need copies of the following picture books by Maurice Sendak:

- *Mr Rabbit and the Lovely Present*
- *Where the Wild Things Are*
- *In the Night Kitchen*
- *Outside Over There*

▶ Read the verbal text of these books to the class without showing any of the illustrations. Be careful not to reveal the front cover of the book at this stage. Ask the students to imagine that they have been commissioned to illustrate one of these texts. They must decide on the style of illustrations that they will use, and justify the reasons for this in terms of the subject and tone of the verbal text.

▶ Allow time for the students to make preliminary sketches, or to collect pictures from other sources, other picture books, magazines, art books and so on. Encourage students to be innovative in the choices they make.

▶ In role as the writer of the story, interview the students/illustrators and explore the reasons for the choices that they have made.

▶ Show the class the covers of each of the four books. Suggest that this is the sort of illustration that you, as the writer, require. Ask them to go back to the drawing board and develop some sketches in this style for parts of the story that they are working on.

▶ Allow time for exploration and discussion of the styles of the covers and the relationship with the stories. Then hold another conference with the 'illustrators' to consider their proposals.

▶ Divide the class into four groups and give each group one of the books to read together.

- ▶ Ask each group to examine the book closely, looking particularly at the nature of the story, the colours used, the style of illustration, the interrelationship between the verbal and visual text, and the tone of the book. Ask each group to consider what the style of the illustrations contributes to the story itself. Compare these with the illustrations that they had proposed. Are there similarities or differences?
- ▶ Encourage the students to write to Maurice Sendak with any queries that they may have about the nature of his illustrations.
- ▶ Encourage the students to research the work of Maurice Sendak to find out about his mode of illustration.
- ▶ Ask the students to imagine that they are Maurice Sendak. They have been commissioned to illustrate some well-known fairy tales, e.g. Hansel and Gretel. What style of illustration would they choose? What aspects of the story suggest this? What understandings of the work of Maurice Sendak suggest this?
- ▶ The students could take on the role of writers of a *Who's Who of Picture Book Illustrators* and write the entry on Maurice Sendak.

Outside Over There by Maurice Sendak.

*A*uthor and *I*llustrator

In this section students are encouraged to explore the ways different authors and illustrators produce different styles of books.

To complete these activities you will need copies of the following picture books:
- *The Tram to Bondi Beach*   Elizabeth Hathorn & Julie Vivas
- *Wilfrid Gordon McDonald Partridge*   Mem Fox & Julie Vivas
- *Guess What?*   Mem Fox & Vivienne Goodman

Guess What? by Mem Fox.

▶ Begin by asking students to consider how an author and illustrator might work together. Which comes first — the words or the pictures? Does the story grow from the discussions between the two storymakers? Can the story develop from the pictures?

▶ Ask students to consider how they would go about selecting an ilustrator for a story they had written. What would be the most important consideration for them in the style of the illustrator?

▶ Ask students to consider how they would go about choosing a writer for a story they had developed through pictures? What would be the most important considerations for them as illustrators? Would the use of a photographer change the way the author might work?

▶ Show the students a variety of picture book titles. Ask them to look closely at the credits on the title pages.
- Have the books been written and illustrated by the same person?
- If there are different people responsible for the visual and verbal texts, how are these accredited?
- Is the writer given prominence?
- Is the illustrator accredited with 'pictures' or 'illustrations'?
- What is the difference between pictures and illustrations?
- What do we value more, pictures or words?

▶ Very often authors and illustrators do not have the option of choosing their collaborators. This may be done by the publisher. Ask the students to consider what considerations a publisher might have in making such a choice.

- ▶ Now show students the work of Julie Vivas in her collaboration with Elizabeth Hathorn in the book *The Tram to Bondi Beach*. Encourage the students to discuss the nature of the story and the ways in which the illustrations contribute to the tone and mood of the tale.
- ▶ Read to the class *Wilfrid Gordon McDonald Partridge* which is written by Mem Fox in collaboration with Julie Vivas. Allow plenty of time to discuss the ways in which the illustrations contribute to the tone and mood of the story.
- ▶ Now read *Guess What?* written by Mem Fox in collaboration with Vivienne Goodman. Allow time to discuss the style of the illustrations in this book. Encourage the students to speculate as to the reasons Mem Fox did not collaborate with Julie Vivas on this book.
- ▶ Ask the students to develop illustrations in the style of Julie Vivas for *Guess What?* and in the style of Vivienne Goodman for *Wilfrid Gordon McDonald Partridge*. What does the changed style do to the tone and mood of the story?
- ▶ Set up some improvisation scenes for the students to explore the interactions that have led to these collaborations, for example:
  - Mem Fox and the publisher discussing *Wilfrid Gordon McDonald Partridge*;
  - Julie Vivas and the publisher discussing this story;
  - Mem Fox and Julie Vivas discussing this story;
  - Mem Fox and the publisher discussing *Guess What?*;
  - Mem Fox and Vivienne Gordon discussing *Guess What?*;
  - Mem Fox, Vivienne Goodman and the publisher after the final manuscript and artwork have been presented.
- ▶ Ask the students to imagine that they are Mem Fox and to write a letter to Julie Vivas explaining the decision to work with Vivienne Goodman on *Guess What?*
- ▶ Ask the students to take on the role of Julie Vivas and reply to the letter.
- ▶ Ask the students to take on the role of Vivienne Goodman and write a letter to Mem Fox outlining why these illustrations would be appropriate to the text.
- ▶ Ask the students to develop a brief outline of a story for a picture book. Then ask them to draft a letter to an illustrator of their choice outlining the style of the illustrations they would like for this picture book.
- ▶ Ask students to present their outline to a publisher with suggestions as to the style of illustrations.
- ▶ Ask students to take on the role of the publisher and reply to this letter.
- ▶ Provide students with the verbal text from a picture book and ask them, in the role of publisher, to write a 'brief' for the illustrator on the style of illustrations that should accompany this verbal text.
- ▶ Encourage the students to research other author/illustrator combinations and the changes that occur when these collaborations are altered.

Wider Reading

In this book, our main concern has been to establish the value of picture books as a genre in themselves. In doing so we have dealt with a rather narrow range of books, authors and illustrators. The purpose of this has been primarily to encourage teachers to get to know some picture books so well that they feel confident in exploring the range further. There is an enormous field to explore.

We have intended to show that picture books can provide readers with a depth and breadth of literary experience, as well as allowing readers to become conscious of their own reading processes. We have also included some picture books that are of a more light-hearted nature, that allow students to simply enjoy words and pictures without necessarily being drawn into a 'deep and meaningful' experience. Moreover, we have been concerned to show that the group reading of a picture book can involve the participants in a valuable, interactive, meaning-making event. This is just as applicable in the secondary school as in the primary school.

Picture books can also be used as a means of exploring other aspects of language and literature in the classroom situation. The section on Shakespeare has demonstrated how some picture books can be used to explore issues relating to some of his plays, as well as explaining some of the structural features of them. Picture books can provide a useful adjunct to the reading of other fiction. The link can be established in a number of ways: thematically, through narrative perspective, through other structural features, and so on.

A thematic approach allows students to explore issues through a number of picture books and then to transfer their understandings to their readings of other narrative fiction. A thematic study that explores issues of gender stereotypes in literature using novels such as *Handles*, or *The Turbulent Term of Tyke Tiler*, could be enhanced by picture books such as *The Paper Bag Princess*, *Princess Smartypants*, *Prince Cinders*, or *Piggybook*. A thematic study about coping with death or loss, based perhaps on novels such as *The Bridge to Terabithia* or *The Great Gilly Hopkins*, could be expanded through a reading of picture books such as *Fred*, *Granpa*, *John Brown, Rose and the Midnight Cat*, *A Cat and Mouse Love Story*, *Rose Blanche*, or *The Children We Remember*.

Picture books may be linked to other fiction reading through such literary aspects as the narrative perspective, or the sequencing of the story. A study of the shifts in narrative perspective in *Granpa*, for instance is an easy way to introduce the narrative shifts that occur in books such as *Breaktime* or *Dance on My Grave*. The use of speech balloons in books such as *Fred* and *Lulu and the Flying Babies* provides an easy link with the interior monologues that occur in a novel such as *Eleanor Elisabeth*.

It is not only to narrative fiction that we can link picture books. We have already demonstrated some links with the study of Shakespeare. The notion of subtext in dramatic literature is readily linked to *Rosie's Walk*, *One Sunday* and *The Story of Chicken Licken*. These picture books can be used to demonstrate the action that is unstated, and this understanding can be transferred to other dramatic literature. *Granpa* provides opportunity to explore voice and dialogue, as well as the alter ego of a character.

The nature of picture books also makes them a useful tool to explore aspects of the media, particularly film or video. Books such as *Crazy Crazy*, or *Fred* are almost in the form of a storyboard. These can be used to stimulate students to think about the nature of camera shots and angles. Students can be encouraged to use these as models for their own storyboards of other narrative fiction.

Good picture books provide a model for students' own writing. Whatever the form, be it poetry, narrative, or dialogue, a good picture book offers students language models that resonate, and these models should enrich students' oral and written language. While the focus in this book has been on using the verbal text of the picture book as a model for similar styles of writing, there are many possibilities for other writing activities. *Granpa* and *Wilfrid Gordon McDonald Partridge*, for instance, can lead into various writing tasks about old age. *Crusher is Coming* or *The Very Worst Monster* can stimulate writing in a variety of forms, about sibling rivalry.

Many picture books are a useful starting point for improvisation or role-play. This is particularly true of the wordless picture books, such as *River* and *Inter-City* and the dual narrative picture books such as *One Sunday*, *Rosie's Walk* and *The Story of Chicken Licken*.

Poetry and picture books go hand in hand. While the language of most picture books is not in a poetic genre, the picture book, by its very nature, is poetic in its compression of imagery. Moreover, some picture books do in fact use poetic forms in their verbal text. This has been demonstrated in the section on poetic language. Apart from the light-hearted rhyming and rhythmic patterns that we have identified, there are many picture books that offer a deeply moving poetic experience. *Owl Moon* is one of many such books.

> When you go owling
> you don't need words
> or warm
> or anything but hope.
> That's what Pa says.
> The kind of hope
> that flies
> on silent wings
> under a shining
> Owl Moon.

SHARING THE JOY

The previous sections may seem to suggest that picture books are the stuff that lessons are made of. They could provide a new study within the classroom to such an extent that students begin to talk about the picture books they are 'doing'. We want to end this book by asserting that the real value of picture books is that they can promote enjoyment of sharing stories. We would not want to see that enjoyment eclipsed by a constant push to study the picture book genre *ad nauseam*.

There are many picture books which provide a deep aesthetic experience for the reader, which is further enhanced by the context of the shared reading experience. Human beings of all ages need story to enrich the human experience. Picture books, by their very nature, allow a variety of ages to enter the story at different stages of reading development. In sharing a picture book with readers who are at different stages, the story experience of all is enriched.

There are times when it is more than sufficient to simply share the reading of a picture book in the classroom: there is in fact no necessity for exercises, for explanations, for oral or written activities. All that is required is the sharing of the story: this in itself constitutes a valuable and moving literary experience, of the kind suggested by the movie *Dead Poet's Society*.

Some picture books lend themselves very well to the shared reading experience. The following list is by no means exhaustive, but is certainly a beginning point.

- *Owl Moon*   Jane Yolen & John Schoenherr
- *The Wreck of the Zephyr*   Chris Van Allsburg
- *The Wedding Ghost*   Leon Garfield & Charles Keeping
- *The Little Red Cap*   Translated by Elizabeth Crawford, illustrated by Lisbeth Zwerger
- *Uhu*   Annette Macarthur-Onslow
- *The Painter and the Wild Swans*   Claude Clement & Frederic Clement
- *The Moon's Revenge*   Joan Aiken & Alan Lee
- *The White Crane*   Junko Morimoto
- *The Mirrorstone*   Michael Palin, Alan Lee & Richard Seymour
- *Rose Blanche*   Roberto Innocenti
- *Through the Window*   Charles Keeping
- *The Bear Who Wanted to Stay a Bear*   Jörg Muller & Jörg Steiner

References

Christie, Michael, J. *Aboriginal Perspectives on Experience and Learning: The Role of Language in Aboriginal Education*. Deakin University, Victoria, 1985.

Cummins, Jim. *Bilingualism and Special Education: Issues in Assessment and Pedagogy*, Multilingual Matters 6. Multilingual Matters Ltd, Great Britain, 1984.

Iser, Wolfgang. *The Act of Reading*. Routledge & Kegan Paul, London, 1978.

Meek, Margaret. *How Texts Teach What Readers Learn*. The Thimble Press in association with the Primary English Teaching Association, NSW, 1989.

NSW Board of Secondary Education. 'English Syllabus, Years 7–10', 1987.

—— 'Contemporary English Syllabus, Years 11–12', 1988.

New South Wales Department of Education. *Communicative Activities— What, Why, How and Where* in 'Topics in ESL—5', 1984.

Thomson, Jack. *Understanding Teenagers' Reading: Reading Processes and the Teaching of Literature*. Methuen Australia, Sydney, 1987.

Victorian Curriculum and Assessment Board. 'English Study Design', 1989.

Bibliography

Books

Alderman, Belle & Harman, Lauren. *The Imagineers*. Reading Time Publication No. 5, ACT, 1983.

Alderman, Belle & Reeder, Stephanie Owen. *The Inside Story: Creating Children's Books*. Children's Book Council of Australia, Canberra, 1987.

Benton, Michael & Fox, Geoff. *Teaching Literature*. Oxford University Press, Oxford, 1985.

Berg, Leila. *Reading and Loving*. Routledge & Kegan Paul, London, 1977.

Berger, John. *Ways of Seeing*. BBC/Penguin, London, 1972.

Carpenter, H. *The Oxford Companion to Children's Literature*. Oxford University Press, Oxford, 1984.

Chambers, Aidan. *Booktalk*. Bodley Head, London, 1985.

Chambers, Nancy. *The Signal Approach to Children's Literature*. Kestrel, London, 1980.

Corcoran, Bill & Evans, Emrys. *Readers, Texts, Teachers*. Boynton/Cook, USA, 1987.

Dugan, Michael. *The Early Dreaming: Australian Children's Authors on Childhood*. Jacaranda Press, Brisbane, 1980.

Davidson, Merrilyn et al. *Moving on with Big Books*. Ashton Scholastic, Gosford, 1989.

Fox, Geoff. *Writers, Critics and Children*. Heinemann, London, 1976.

Hancock, Joelie & Hill, Susan. *Literature-based Reading Programs at Work*. ARA, Melbourne, 1987.

Hanzl, Anne (Ed). *Literature: A Focus for Language Learning*. ARA, Melbourne, 1988.

Hoogstad, Valerie & Saxby, Maurice. *Teaching Literature to Adolescents*. Nelson, Melbourne, 1988.

Inglis, Fred. *The Promise of Happiness: Value and Meaning in Children's*

Literature. Cambridge University Press, Cambridge, 1981.

Ingram, Anne Bower & Graham, B. *Making a Picture Book*. Nelson, Melbourne, 1987.

Kirkpatrick, D. L. (Ed). *Twentieth Century Children's Writers*. Macmillan, London, 1978.

Lanes, Selma. *The Art of Maurice Sendak*. Bodley Head, London, 1980.

McVitty, Walter. *Innocence and Experience*. Nelson, Melbourne, 1981.

McVitty, Walter (Ed). *The PETA Guide to Children's Literature*. PETA, Sydney, 1985.

Meek, Margaret. *Achieving Literacy*. Routledge & Kegan Paul, London, 1983.

Meek, Margaret et al. *The Cool Web: The Pattern of Children's Reading*. Bodley Head, London, 1977.

Muir, Marcie. *A History of Australian Children's Book Illustration*. Oxford University Press, Melbourne, 1982.

Niall, Brenda. *Australia Through the Looking Glass: Children's Fiction 1830–1980*. Melbourne University Press, Melbourne, 1984.

O'Sullivan, Colleen. *The Challenge of Picture Books*. Methuen, Sydney, 1987.

Reid, Ian. *The Making of Literature*. Australian Association for the Teaching of English, 1984.

Robertson, Marion E. & Poston Anderson, Barbara. *Readers Theatre*. Hodder and Stoughton, Sydney, 1986.

Rosen, Betty. *And None of it Was Nonsense*. Scholastic, Canada, 1988.

Rosenblatt, Louise. *The Reader, the Text, the Poem*. Southern Illinois Press, Carbondale, 1978.

Sawyer, Ruth. *The Way of the Storyteller*. Bodley Head, London, 1962.

Saxby, M. & Winch, G. *Give Them Wings*. Macmillan, Melbourne, 1987.

Saxby, H. M. *A History of Australian Children's Literature: Vol. 1 1841–1941*. Wentworth Books, Sydney, 1969.

———. *Vol. 2 1941–1970*. Wentworth Books, Sydney, 1971.

Saxby, Maurice (Ed). *Through Folklore to Literature*. IBBY Australia Publications, Sydney, 1979.

Schmidt, Janine. *Australian Picture Books*. Kuringai College of Advanced Education, Lindfield, 1984.

Smith, Frank. *Reading*. University of Cambridge, Cambridge, 1978.

Stodart, Eleanor. *Writing and Illustrating for Children*. Children's Book Council of Australia, Seminars 1975–1980, Canberra, 1985.

Thomas, R. & Perry, A. *Into Books*. Oxford University Press, Melbourne, 1984.

Townsend, John Rowe. *Written for Children*. Penguin, London, 1987.

Townsend, John Rowe. *A Sense of Story*. Kestrel, London, 1979.

Trelease, Jim. *The Read Aloud Handbook*. Australian Adaptation by Moira Robinson, Penguin, Melbourne, 1986.

Tucker, Nicholas. *The Child and the Book*. Cambridge University Press, Cambridge, 1981.

Walshe, R. D., Jensen, D. & Moore, T. *Teaching Literature*. PETA & ETA, Sydney, 1983.

Walker, Maxine. *Writers Alive! Current Australian Authors for Children*. Westbooks, Perth, 1977.

Watson, K. (Ed). *Reading is Response*. St Clair Press, Sydney, 1980.

White, Mary Lou. *Children's Literature: Criticism and Response*. Merrill, Columbus, 1976.

Winch, G. & Hoogstad, V. *Teaching Reading*. Macmillan, Melbourne, 1985.

Periodicals and Journals

Bookbird
Children's Literature in Education
Growing Point
Horn Book
Junior Bookshelf
Language Arts
Magpies
Orana
Reading Time
Signal
Top of the News

Acknowledgements

The authors and publisher would like to thank the following for permission to reproduce copyright material:

Illustrations

Andersen Press, UK, p. 48; Angus & Robertson Publishers, p. 47; Annick Press Ltd, Toronto, p. 71, from *The Paper Bag Princess* written by Robert Munsch, illustrated by Michael Martchenko, reprinted with permission; The Bodley Head, UK, pp 16, 84, 95, 110, reprinted with permission of Maurice Sendak, p. 8, reprinted with permission of Pat Hutchins; Jonathan Cape, p. 10, reproduced with permission of Posy Simmonds, p. 17, reprinted with permission of John Burningham; Collins Publishers, pp 77, 79; Hamish Hamilton Ltd, UK, pp 33, 68, 73, 106; William Heinemann Ltd, UK, p. 34; Janet and Andrew McLean, p. 43; Methuen Children's Books Ltd, UK, p. 42; Omnibus Books, pp 76, 81, 100, 104, 111; Oxford University Press, UK, pp 5, 19, 44, 56, 58, 63, 90; Penguin Books Ltd, p. 55; Penguin Books Australia Ltd, pp 22, 40; Julia MacRae Books, pp 12, 25, 31, 38.

Text

Angus & Robertson Publishers, p. 46, from Libby Gleeson & John Winch, *One Sunday*, 1988; Ashton Scholastic, p. 114, from *Owl Moon*, text © Jane Yolen 1987, illustrations © John Schoenherr 1987, published by arrangement with Putnam Publishing Group; Collins Publishers, p. 76, from Percy Trezise & Dick Roughsey, *The Quinkins*, 1985; Hamish Hamilton Ltd, UK, p. 69, from Anthony Browne, *Bear Hunt*, 1979; Methuen Australia, p. 27, from Jack Thomson, *Understanding Teenagers' Reading*, 1987, pp 360–1; Penguin Books Ltd, p. 45, from Pat Hutchins, *Rosie's Walk*, Picture Puffin, 1970.

Disclaimer

Every effort has been made to trace the original source of copyright material contained in this book. The publisher would be pleased to hear from copyright holders to rectify any errors or omissions.

General Index

Index of Picture Books

For ease of use the picture books in this index are listed alphabetically by title rather than by author as in a bibliography.

123